CONTENTS

INTRODUCTION 8

BLACKSTONE OUTDOOR GAS GRIDDLE BASICS 10

Blackstone Outdoor Gas Griddle 10

Seasoning Your Blackstone Griddle.. 11

Essential Tools for Griddle 12

Benefits of Using Blackstone Outdoor Gas Griddle 12

How to Store and Maintain Your Seasoned Griddle Properly? 13

PRO TIPS 14

BREAKFAST 17

Almond Pancakes 17

French Toast Sticks 17

Simple Cheese Sandwich 18

Cauliflower Fritters 18

Easy Banana Pancakes 19

Cauliflower Hash Browns 19

Tomato Scrambled Egg 20

Caprese Omelet 20

Pumpkin Pancake 21

Easy Cheese Omelet 21

Spinach Pancakes 22

Spicy Egg Scrambled 22

Chocolate Pancake 23

Broccoli Omelet 23

Healthy Oatmeal Pancake 24

BREAKFAST SANDWICHES & BREADS 25

Tangy Chicken Sandwiches 25

Savory Chicken Burgers 26

Sun-Dried Tomato and Chicken Flatbreads 27

Turkey Pesto Panini 28

Classic American Burger 29

Layered Beef & Corn Burger 30

Pork Tenderloin Sandwiches 31

Cheesy Ham and Pineapple Sandwich 31

Croque Madame 32

Salmon Burgers 33

Ultimate Griddle Cheese 33

Garlic Parmesan Griddle Cheese Sandwiches 34

Griddle Pizza Cheese 35

Mini Portobello Burgers 36

Veggie Pesto Flatbread 37

Griddle Vegetable Pizza 38

Bacon Jalapeno Wraps 38

MAIN DISHES: PORK **39**

Pork Tenderloin Sandwiches 39

Herb-Crusted Mediterranean Pork Tenderloin 40

Paprika Dijon Pork Tenderloin 41

Moroccan Spiced Pork Tenderloin with Creamy Harissa Sauce 42

Sticky-Sweet Pork Shoulder 43

Griddle Pork Chops with Herb Apple Compote 44

Yucatan-Style Griddle Pork 45

Glazed Country Ribs 46

Pineapple Bacon Pork Chops 47

Habanero-Marinated Pork Chops 48

Garlic Soy Pork Chops 49

Honey Soy Pork Chops 49

Cuban Pork Chops 50

Spicy Cajun Pork Chops 50

MAIN DISHES: POULTRY **51**

Classic BBQ Chicken 51

California Seared Chicken 52

Sweet Chili Lime Chicken 53

Seared Spicy Citrus Chicken 54

Honey Balsamic Marinated Chicken 55

Salsa Verde Marinated Chicken 56

Hasselback Stuffed Chicken 57

Creole Chicken Stuffed with Cheese & Peppers 58

Root Beer Can Chicken 59

Chipotle Adobe Chicken 60

Chicken Tacos with Avocado Crema 61

Sizzling Chicken Fajitas 62

Hawaiian Chicken Skewers 63

Fiery Italian Chicken Skewers 64

Chicken Thighs with Ginger-Sesame Glaze 65

Honey Sriracha Griddle Chicken Thighs 66

Buffalo Chicken Wings 67

Chicken Wings with Sweet Red Chili and Peach Glaze 68

Yellow Curry Chicken Wings 68

Korean Griddle Chicken Wings with Scallion 69

Kale Caesar Salad with Seared Chicken 70

Seared Chicken with Fruit Salsa 71

Teriyaki Chicken and Veggie Rice Bowls 72

Chicken Satay with Almond Butter Sauce 73

Chicken Fried Rice 74

TURKEY RECIPES **75**

Herb Roasted Turkey 75

Turkey Legs 76

Turkey Breast 77

Smoked Whole Turkey 78

Savory-Sweet Turkey Legs 79

Marinated Smoked Turkey Breast 80

Maple Bourbon Turkey 81

Thanksgiving Turkey 82

Spatchcock Smoked Turkey 83

Hoisin Turkey Wings 84

Turkey Jerky 85

Smoked Whole Turkey 86

Smoked Turkey Breast 87

Whole Turkey 88

Herbed Turkey Breast 89

Jalapeno Injection Turkey 90

Smoked Turkey Mayo with Green Apple 91

Buttery Smoked Turkey Beer 92

Barbecue Chili Smoked Turkey Breast 93

Hot Sauce Smoked Turkey Tabasco 94

Cured Turkey Drumstick 95

Tailgate Smoked Young Turkey 96

Roast Turkey Orange 97

MAIN DISHES: SEAFOOD **98**

Salmon Fillets with Basil Butter & Broccolini 98

Spiced Snapper with Mango and Red Onion Salad 99

Honey-Lime Tilapia and Corn Foil Pack 100

Halibut Fillets with Spinach and Olives 100

Gremolata Swordfish Skewers 101

Lobster Tails with Lime Basil Butter 102

Spiced Crab Legs 102

Lump Crab Cakes 103

Spicy Griddle Jumbo Shrimp 103

Coconut Pineapple Shrimp Skewers 104

Mexican Shrimp Tacos 105

Bacon Wrapped Scallops 106

Scallops with Lemony Salsa Verde 106

Griddle Oysters with Spiced Tequila Butter 107

Pop-Open Clams with Horseradish-Tabasco Sauce 108

Spicy Griddle Squid 109

VEGETABLE & SIDE DISHES **110**

Stir Fry Mushrooms 110

Stir Fry Vegetables 110

Easy Fried Rice 111

Healthy Zucchini Noodles 111

Easy Seared Green Beans 112

Stir Fry Bok Choy 112

Sautéed Vegetables 113

Stir Fry Cabbage 113

Pineapple Fried Rice 114

Italian Zucchini Slices 114

GAME RECIPES **115**

Flavorful Cornish Game Hen 115

Flavorful Marinated Cornish Hen 115

Montreal Seasoned Spatchcocked Hens 116

Rosemary Hen 116

BBQ Hen 117

Honey Garlic Cornish Hen 117

Sage Thyme Cornish Hen 118

Asian Cornish Hen 118

Orange Cornish Hen 119

Rosemary Butter Cornish Hens 120

APPETIZERS AND SIDES RECIPES **121**

Smashed Potato Casserole 121

Atomic Buffalo Turds 122

Brisket Baked Beans 123

Twice-Baked Spaghetti Squash 124

Bacon-Wrapped Asparagus 125

Garlic Parmesan Wedges 126

Smoked Moink Ball Skewers 127

Bacon Cheddar Slider 128

Mushrooms Stuffed with Crab Meat 129

Parmesan Tomatoes.. 130

Feta Spinach Turkey Burgers.. 131

Griddle Potato Skewers 132

Curried Cauliflower Skewers 133

Southwest Chicken Drumsticks 133

Sweet Potato Fries 134

Balsamic Mushroom Skewers 134

DESSERT AND SNACKS RECIPES **135**

Spicy Sausage & Cheese Balls... 135

White Chocolate Bread Pudding 136

Cheesy Jalapeño Griddle Dip 137

Cajun Turkey Club 138

Juicy Loosey Cheeseburger 139

No Flip Burgers 140

Juicy Loosey Smokey Burger.. 140

Bread Pudding 141

Smoked Chocolate Bacon Pecan Pie 142

Bacon Sweet Potato Pie 143

Griddle Fruit with Cream 144

Apple Pie on the Griddle 145

Griddle Layered Cake 145

Coconut Chocolate Simple Brownies 146

Seasonal Fruit on the Griddle 146

Bacon Chocolate Chip Cookies 147

Chocolate Chip Cookies 148

Apple Cobbler 149

Caramel Bananas 150

Cinnamon Sugar Pumpkin Seeds 150

Blackberry Pie 151

S'mores Dip 152

Ice Cream Bread 152

30 DAY MEAL PLAN **153**

INTRODUCTION

The Blackstone Flat Top Griddle provides 720 inches of professional grade griddle for your back yard or really anywhere you go. Now, you can make professional quality meals and get the same results professional chefs achieve every time you cook. The Blackstone Flat Top Griddle is designed to produce perfectly even and adjustable heat over four different cooking zones, so you can always have the exact temperature you need at a moment's notice.

The Blackstone Flat Top Griddle is made with professional grade materials and provides professional quality heat in the form of 60,000 BTU of cooking power with four independent cooking zones. This means you can carefully control everything you cook with individual controls for each zone. Eggs don't cook properly at the same temperature as a steak, and the Blackstone Griddle allows you to cook both, perfectly, at the same time.

Are you an avid camper? Do you love to tailgate before the big game? Do you like to cook at friends' houses? Well, the Blackstone Griddle allows you maximum flexibility by letting you take your griddle wherever you need to go. With minimal effort you can remove the flat top, safely fold and stow the legs, and remove the propane tank. Best of all, the griddle comes with industrial grade casters so you can roll the griddle wherever it needs to go.

Because it's built from industrial grade materials, your Blackstone Griddle will be a versatile appliance for many years to come. The frame of the griddle is built with super durable powder coated steel. The burners are made from restaurant grade stainless steel and are guaranteed to produce perfectly even and powerful heat for years to come. Once you've spent some time with your Blackstone Griddle you might even consider getting rid of your more conventional gas or charcoal grills.

Say goodbye to dirty charcoal and matches forever. Charcoal is dirty, expensive, and harmful to your health, so why are you still using it? The Blackstone Griddle uses a standard refillable propane tank which attaches to the griddle with ease. And thanks to the simple push button ignitor, starting your griddle is as easy as pushing a button.

Who is it Good For?

Because the Blackstone Griddle is large enough to cook all the parts of a complete meal at the same time, it is perfect for families who love perfectly prepared backyard favorites like burgers, steaks, and veggies, but it's also perfect for families who love to make big breakfasts. Prepare eggs, bacon, hash browns, and pancakes for everyone at the same time.

Do you love to cook big meals on the go? The Blackstone Griddle is perfect for camping and tailgating because of how easy it is to transport and set up. Pack it up for your next camping trip and set it up when you want to make an amazing outdoor meal. The Griddle is also perfect for anyone who loves making fresh grilled food for a professional tailgate party. Since the Griddle easily fits in the trunk of a car, you can take it with you to the game and set it up in minutes. Impress the whole parking lot with the amazing food you make for your fellow fans.

Who is it NOT Good For?

Everyone loves food cooked in the open air, but if you don't have a large enough outdoor space in which to use the Griddle, this may not be for you. A good rule of thumb is that you can use the griddle anywhere you would use a conventional gas or charcoal grill.

A Few Cautions

Because the Blackstone Griddle uses an external propane tank, you will want to exercise caution while connecting and disconnecting the tank. Always make sure all connection points are clean and free of debris. When attaching the hose to the tank, make sure the valve is completely tight before allowing gas to flow to the griddle.

The Blackstone Griddle's cold rolled steel flat top produces amazing results, but because it gets very hot, you should make sure children are always supervised when near the griddle.

BLACKSTONE OUTDOOR GAS GRIDDLE BASICS

Blackstone Outdoor Gas Griddle

Blackstone is a leading manufacturer of outdoor griddle which improves your outdoor cooking experience. They are one of the top industry leader's manufactures in the USA made outdoor gas griddles since 2005. The Blackstone outdoor griddle or grills are one of the best-selling flagship products available in the USA market.

The Blackstone outdoor gas griddle is one of the best affordable gas griddle devices compare to other devices available in the market. It is available in two different sizes one is 28 inch and the other is 36-inch size. The 28-inch gas griddle made up of stainless-steel frame comes with a 470 square inch cooking surface area. The gas griddle is loaded with two H-shape large size gas burners each burner can produce 15000 BTU and both the burner's together produce 30000 BTU heat. The 36-inch gas griddle offers a 720 square inch large size cooking area to cook a whole family food at a time. The gas griddle is loaded with four H-shape large size gas burners. All together these burners can produce 6000 BTU of heat. All the burners are equipped with separate controller switch so you can easily controller them independently.

The Blackstone gas griddle is easy to assemble and built up with high-quality stainless steel coated with black powder coating. The main cooking surface area is made up of thick rolled steel material. The griddle has a battery power ignition system started by just push-button ignition and capable to produce a maximum 350 °F temperature. The four heavy-duty burners heat-up the cooking area very fast. The Blackstone gas griddle comes with a bottom shelf and two convenient side-mounted shelves and a propane tank holder. You can easily move the gas griddle outdoor cooking appliance with the help of four caster wheels. You can lock two wheels among these four wheels to keep your appliance steady in your backyard.

Its large 720 square inches cooking surface area is capable to handle a large quantity of food. It is capable to hold 16 steaks, 72 hot dogs, and 28 hamburgers at a time. It is also capable to cook two different foods at the same time but on different temperature settings. When you cook eggs, it is not suitable to cook it at 60000BTU heat but at the same temperature settings is suitable for steak. The griddle allows you to individually control all four heating zones as per your recipe needs at the same time.

Seasoning Your Blackstone Griddle

When you buy a new griddle, it is recommended that before using the griddle season it with proper seasoning method to make a non-stick layer over the cooking area and avoid scratching while cooking your food. You just need to follow the simple seasoning steps given below to improve your griddle cooking efficiency. Before starting seasoning make sure you have collected all items and supplies needed during the seasoning process. These items and supplies include a Bucket of water, tongs or heatproof gloves, soap powder, salt, stick, and cast-iron conditioner.

1. Clean your brand-new griddle with soapy water

Take 2 liters of warm water into a bucket and some soap. Mix the soap and water solution with the help of a stick. Then pour a small amount of soapy water over the griddle cooking surface and thoroughly rub it over the griddle surface with the help of a paper towel.

If you are using an old griddle then skip this soapy water step this step may damage the coating area of the griddle.

2. Heat the griddle for 10 t0 15 minutes

Turn on all the burners with its maximum temperature settings and allow the griddle heat up for 10 to 15 minutes. After some time, you will notice that the top of the griddle turns brown. Then move to the next step.

3. Spread oil over griddle surface

You can choose your favorite oil for seasoning griddle. Always use high fatty acid oil like extra virgin olive oil, vegetable oil, coconut oil, flaxseed oil, and more to coat your griddle. Take 2 to 3 tablespoon of oil and spread them over the griddle surface. Use a paper towel to spread the oil equally all over the griddle surface. You can also use a highly recommended cast iron conditioner for the coating griddle surface. Then move to the next step.

4. Fire the griddle again

Ignite all the burners at its max temperature position and allow it for 15 to 30 minutes at max setting. You will notice the griddle turns black after some time and the oil begin smoking when it reaches its smoke point. Wait until the smoke will completely disappear.

5. Turn of griddle

Turn off the griddle after completing the first cycle and let it cool down at least 10 minutes. After that repeat the same procedure again and again until the griddle is turned dark brown. It requires 3 to 4 repetitions.

6. Final touch

Wipe the griddle with high quality extra virgin oil or cast-iron conditioner to prevent it from oxidation. Now your griddle seasoning process is completed successfully.

Essential Tools for Griddle

Three main necessary tools make you master in griddle cooking. These tools are oil bottles, Spatula, and Scrapers which makes outdoor griddle cooking easy. You can also use extra tools if you want to baste, steam, press, and blacken your food.

1. Spatula

It is one of the necessary tools used to flip, spread, mix, and lift your favorite foods like pancakes, burgers, eggs, veggies, omelets, and more. It is one kind of flat, broad, and flexible tool with an ergonomic handle made up of sturdy stainless-steel material and available in large, medium, and small sizes.

2. Scraper

Scraper is a sharp blade-like tool used to clean your griddle surface for derbies. The scraper is a wide stainless-steel blade comes with an ergonomic sleep resistant grip which provides perfect control when scrapping and digging over a griddle.

3. Squeeze Bottles

Squeeze bottles are easy tools to spread oils, sausage, and water while griddles your food. The squeeze bottles are made up of high-quality BPA-free plastic.

4. Round Basting Cover

The blasting cover is made up of stainless-steel material and comes with a safety handle. A blasting cover is a multipurpose tool used to steam veggies, melting cheese, and more. Use a 12-inch big-size blasting cover that is capable to hold a large portion of your food and number of patties at a time.

5. Bacon Grill Press

The grill press is made up of cast iron and comes with a wooden handle grip for safety purposes. It is idle for making flatten bacon, hamburgers, sandwiches, and also used as a steak weight. The main purpose of using a press grill is to remove out excess grease from burgers.

Benefits of Using Blackstone Outdoor Gas Griddle

There are lots of benefits to cooking your food on a Blackstone outdoor gas griddle. Let's see all these benefits one by one.

1. Large and Flat Surface Cooking

One of the main benefits of the Blackstone gas griddle is its large and flat cooking surface. The large cooking area allows you to cook more food items to cook at once and flip food is easy to compare to a frying pan. You can use the griddle to cook a large quantity of food. The Blackstone griddle is capable to hold 72 hotdogs, 28 hamburgers, and 16 steaks in a single cooking batch. Due to the large cooking surface, it doesn't hold moisture and gives you a crispy cooking result. It is one of the perfect choices for bigger families who love to enjoy food like eggs, bacon, hotdogs, burgers, and veggies at the same time in backyard parties.

2. Excellent built quality

The Blackstone gas grills are made up of high-quality stainless-steel materials. The main cooking surface is made up of rolled high quality 7-gauge steel. The entire body surface is covered with a black powder coating which protects it from rust.

3. Runs on Propane gas

The Blackstone gas grills use propane gas to cook your food. Compare to charcoal fuel propane gas never creates smoke and harmful gases while cooking food in your backyard. Propane griddles are easy to start all you just need to turn the dial and the burner fired up. The gas griddle is capable to maintain a steady temperature. Your griddle takes less than 15 minutes to reaches its maximum temperature.

4. Versatile

The Blackstone gas griddle is one of the versatile outdoor cooking appliances offers to cook most of the foods over a smooth cooking surface. The Blackstone gas griddle is equipped with 4 burners which allow you to operate them individually. The griddle is capable to cook different types of food at a different temperature at the same time. You can make pancakes, eggs, waffles, steak, burgers, hot dogs, and more with perfection on Blackstone gas griddle.

5. Easy to clean

To clean the Blackstone griddle is one of the easy tasks you just need to clean the greasy cooking area. To clean grease you can use a spatula or griddle to scrap up grease. Use a paper towel to wipe the cooking surface and finally give the touch-up with a scouring pad.

How to Store and Maintain Your Seasoned Griddle Properly?

The proper storage and maintenance are necessary to increase the lifespan of your griddle. The following steps guide you for the storage and maintenance of your griddle.

1. After each use clean your griddle

When you start using your griddle it seasons automatically after each use. Cleaning is one of the important steps to keep your griddle clean and hygiene. Use hot water and a paper towel to clean the griddle surface. Do not use soapy water to clean the cooking surface use scrapper to clean the cooking area. You can clean the greasy surface with clean and dry paper towels.

2. Remove Rust

If you find any rust spot over the griddle then use 40 or 60 low grit sandpaper or you can also use steel wool to remove the rust spot scrub them properly.

3. Coat griddle after cleaning

After finishing the cleaning process give a thin coat of cooking spray over the griddle cooking surface to prevent rusting built up the overcooking surface area of the griddle.

4. Store and Maintain griddle

After finishing all the cleaning steps store your griddle in a cool and dry place. To prevent dust always keep your griddle into cover and keep it away from the humid area.

PRO TIPS

Season the Cooking Surface

Like most high-quality cooking appliances, the cold rolled steel cooking surface of your Blackstone Griddle needs to be properly seasoned to ensure optimal cooking results. So, you may be asking, "what is seasoning?" Before non-stick coatings existed, there was only one way to make sure food didn't stick to the cooking surface. By creating a layer of burnt on oil, you will not only achieve a perfect non-stick surface, you will also protect the cooking surface from scratches and oxidation. Let's get started. First, use soap and water to thoroughly wash the cooking surface. Use a cloth to dry the surface. Next, apply a small amount of oil to the cooking surface. The best oils to use are those with a high smoke point like vegetable or canola. Use a paper towel to spread the oil evenly across the cooking surface. Turn on all four burners and set the temperature to 275°F. Wait until the oil begins to smoke and the surface begins to darken. Once it is smoking, turn off the burners and allow the griddle to cool. Repeat this process two to three more times until the entire surface is evenly dark. Now your griddle is naturally non-stick and protected from damage and rust.

Keep your Griddle Working from Season to Season

Because you are most likely going to keep your griddle outside, you will need to make sure to do a few things before you store it and before you use it again after being stored. Before you store, make sure to disconnect the gas tank and store away from the griddle with a cap on the valve. You can also purchase a cover for the griddle to keep out insects and dust. When you are ready to start using your griddle again, make sure to check the burner area for spider webs. Webs are flammable and can cause flare ups if you do not clean them out before cooking. Check the level in your gas tank to make sure you have enough fuel to start cooking. Once the tank is attached and you are ready to cook, it's a good idea to perform a new season on the cooking surface. Simply follow the instructions above and your griddle will be good as new.

The Best Way to Clean Your Griddle

After each use you will want to clean your griddle, but your griddle should not be cleaned like regular pots and pans. Since you want to build up a nice coating of seasoning to protect your griddle and get the best possible results, you need to make sure not to use things like dish soap to clean the cooking surface. Most detergents have a grease cutting ingredient and this will eat right through your layer of seasoning. The best way to clean your griddle is the way the pros do in restaurants: with a griddle scraper and hot water. You can purchase a griddle scraper which is designed to get rid of any bits of food left behind without sacrificing the seasoning layer you've achieved. To remove things like fat or sauces, a wash with very hot water will dissolve most things, which you can then scrape away. While you don't have to season your griddle after every cleaning, continuous seasoning will ensure that your griddle stays dark and shiny.

Invest in the Proper Tools

Since the Blackstone Griddle is a professional grade piece of equipment, you should have professional grade cooking tools to get the most out of it. While you may have an array of spatulas in the kitchen, to get the best out of your griddle, we recommend buying two long metal spatulas. These spatulas are not only durable, they allow you to transport and flip a large amount of food at the same time. They are also thin and flexible so you can scoop up things like a whole hash brown without dropping anything. Also recommended are at least one pair of long handled metal tongs which will allow you to reach anywhere on the griddle without worrying about getting burned.

Try Different Cooking Fats

Unlike a traditional griddle which allows any cooking fat to fall onto the coals or gas jets, the Blackstone Griddle keeps your cooking fat right where you want it: on your food! Because of this, you can experiment with different flavors of cooking fat to optimize your results. Different oils impart different flavors, but they also work differently from each other. Olive oil imparts a robust and sometimes spicy black pepper flavor that gives an extra richness to food. The problem with olive oil, however, is that is has a pretty low smoke point, which means that over a certain temperature, the oil will start to taste burned. Use olive oil for foods you are cooking at lower to medium temperature, but avoid it for foods cooked over high heat. If you're looking for oil for high heat cooking, try canola or regular vegetable oil. They will allow you to cook to high heats without that unpleasant burnt taste. And of course, butter packs more flavor than almost anything, but it also has a tendency to burn; so, use butter for low heat cooking or for foods you plan to cook quickly.

The Ultimate Burger

For centuries, mankind has quested after the perfect burger. Since its invention, burger chefs have argued about the best way to grind it; the best way to form the patties; and of course, the best way to cook it. Some say you have to use fancy waygu beef imported from Japan, some say the best method is high heat over charcoal. Well, we're going to put the debate to rest once and for all. The first key to the best burger you've ever had is fat content. If you go to your local supermarket you usually have a choice between 20 percent fat or 10 percent fat. For the perfect burger, this will not do. The perfect burger has between 25 and 30 percent fat, and the best way to achieve this is to grind it yourself using a combination of chuck and short rib. If you don't feel like doing this at home, talk to your local butcher and tell them that you need ground beef with a higher fat content. Also, but sure to always use freshly ground beef. The longer it's sitting in packaging the more compressed it's getting, and compressed beef is the enemy of the perfect burger.

Once you have the right beef, form it into loose balls about 1/3 of a pound. Don't work it too much, and don't press it together, as you want the balls to just barely hold together. Light your griddle and turn the burners to medium heat. You might think that burgers cook best at high heat, but this is wrong. You want to give your burgers time to let their fat render and develop a nice flavorful sear. If you cook too fast, you'll end up with overcooked burgers that are chewy inside. Drizzle a little vegetable oil on the griddle and place the ball on the griddle. Using a griddle weight, press down to "smash" the burger as flat as you'd like. Don't reshape it, just let it press onto the griddle and sprinkle with salt. Use your thumb to make an indentation in the center of the burger so that it stays flat. When the first side has developed a nice sear, flip, season with salt and cook for an equal amount of time. This way your burger will have the time to render its fat and reabsorb it as it cooks. When you've reached the temperature you prefer, remove it from the griddle and allow it to rest for five minutes. Top it however you'd like and enjoy what will be the best burger you've ever had.

BREAKFAST

Almond Pancakes

Preparation Time: 10 minutes
Cooking Time: 10 minutes
Serve: 2

INGREDIENTS:

- 1 egg
- 1/2 cup almond flour
- 1/2 tsp baking powder
- 1/2 tbsp heavy whipping cream
- 1 1/2 tbsp Swerve

DIRECTIONS:

1. Preheat the griddle to medium-low heat.
2. In a bowl, mix almond flour, Baking powder, sweetener, and salt.
3. In another bowl, whisk egg and heavy whipping cream.
4. Add dry ingredients into the wet and mix well.
5. Spray griddle top with cooking spray.
6. Drop batter onto the hot griddle top.
7. Cook pancakes until lightly golden brown from both sides.
8. Serve and enjoy.

NUTRITIONAL: Value (Amount per Serving):Calories 90 Fat 7 g Carbohydrates 13 g Sugar 11 Protein 4 g Cholesterol 87 mg

French Toast Sticks

Preparation Time: 10 minutes
Cooking Time: 10 minutes
Serve: 2

INGREDIENTS:

- 2 eggs
- 4 bread slices, cut each bread slice into 3 pieces vertically
- 2/3 cup milk
- 1/4 tsp ground cinnamon
- 1 tsp vanilla

DIRECTIONS:

1. Preheat the griddle to medium-low heat.
2. In a bowl, whisk eggs with cinnamon, vanilla, and milk.
3. Spray griddle top with cooking spray.
4. Dip each bread piece into the egg mixture and coat well.
5. Place coated bread pieces onto the hot griddle top and cook until golden brown from both sides.
6. Serve and enjoy.

NUTRITIONAL: Value (Amount per Serving): Calories 166 Fat 7 g Carbohydrates 14 g Sugar 5 g Protein 10.4 g Cholesterol 193 mg

Simple Cheese Sandwich

Preparation Time: 10 minutes
Cooking Time: 10 minutes
Serve: 1

INGREDIENTS:

- 2 bread slices
- 2 tsp butter
- 2 cheese slices

DIRECTIONS:

1. Preheat the griddle to medium-low heat.
2. Place cheese slices on top of one bread slice and cover cheese with another bread slice.
3. Spread butter on top of both the bread slices.
4. Place sandwich on hot griddle top and cook until golden brown or until cheese is melted.
5. Serve and enjoy.

NUTRITIONAL: Value (Amount per Serving): Calories 340 Fat 26 g Carbohydrates 9.8 g Sugar 1 g Protein 15.4 g Cholesterol 79 mg

Cauliflower Fritters

Preparation Time: 10 minutes
Cooking Time: 15 minutes
Serve: 6

INGREDIENTS:

- 2 eggs
- 1 large head cauliflower, cut into florets
- 1 tbsp butter
- 1/2 tsp turmeric
- 1 tbsp nutritional yeast
- 2/3 cup almond flour
- 1/4 tsp black pepper
- 1/2 tsp salt

DIRECTIONS:

1. Add cauliflower florets to a large pot.
2. Pour enough water to cover the cauliflower florets. Bring to boil for 8-10 minutes.
3. Drain cauliflower well and transfer in food processor and process until it looks like rice.
4. Transfer cauliflower rice into the large bowl.
5. Add remaining ingredients except for butter to the bowl and stir to combine.
6. Preheat the griddle to medium heat.
7. Melt butter onto the hot griddle top.
8. Make small patties from cauliflower mixture and place on hot griddle top and cook for 3-4 minutes on each side or until lightly golden brown.
9. Serve and enjoy.

NUTRITIONAL: Value (Amount per Serving): Calories 155 Fat 10 g Carbohydrates 11.1 g Sugar 3.9 g Protein 8.1 g Cholesterol 60 mg

Easy Banana Pancakes

Preparation Time: 10 minutes
Cooking Time: 10 minutes
Serve: 6

INGREDIENTS:

- 2 eggs
- 2 tbsp vanilla protein powder
- 1 large banana, mashed
- 1/8 tsp baking powder

DIRECTIONS:

1. Preheat the griddle to medium-low heat.
2. Meanwhile, add all ingredients into the bowl and mix well until combined.
3. Spray griddle top with cooking spray.
4. Pour 3 tablespoons of batter onto hot griddle top to make a pancake.
5. Cook pancake until lightly browned from both sides.
6. Serve and enjoy.

NUTRITIONAL: Value (Amount per Serving): Calories 79 Fat 1.6 g Carbohydrates 5.5 g Sugar 3 g Protein 11 g Cholesterol 55 mg

Cauliflower Hash Browns

Preparation Time: 10 minutes
Cooking Time: 10 minutes
Serve: 6

INGREDIENTS:

- 1 egg
- 3 cups cauliflower, grated
- 3/4 cup cheddar cheese, shredded
- 1/8 tsp pepper
- 1/4 tsp garlic powder
- 1/4 tsp cayenne pepper
- 1/2 tsp salt

DIRECTIONS:

1. Preheat the griddle to medium-low heat.
2. Add all ingredients into the bowl and mix well.
3. Spray griddle top with cooking spray.
4. Make 6 hash browns from mixture and place on hot griddle top and cook until golden brown from both sides.
5. Serve and enjoy.

NUTRITIONAL: Value (Amount per Serving): Calories 80 Fat 5 g Carbohydrates 3 g Sugar 1 g Protein 5 g Cholesterol 46 mg

Tomato Scrambled Egg

Preparation Time: 10 minutes

Cooking Time: 5 minutes

Serve: 2

INGREDIENTS:

- 2 eggs, lightly beaten
- 2 tbsp fresh basil, chopped
- 1 tbsp olive oil
- 1/2 tomato, chopped
- Pepper
- Salt

DIRECTIONS:

1. Preheat the griddle to medium heat.
2. Add oil on top of the griddle.
3. Add tomatoes and cook until softened.
4. Whisk eggs with basil, pepper, and salt.
5. Pour egg mixture on top of tomatoes and cook until eggs are set.
6. Serve and enjoy.

NUTRITIONAL: Value (Amount per Serving): Calories 125 Fat 12 g Carbohydrates 1 g Sugar 0.8 g Protein 5.8 g Cholesterol 164 mg

Caprese Omelet

Preparation Time: 10 minutes

Cooking Time: 10 minutes

Serve: 2

INGREDIENTS:

- 6 eggs
- 3 oz cherry tomatoes, cut in halves
- 1 tbsp fresh basil
- 5 oz mozzarella cheese, sliced
- Pepper
- Salt

DIRECTIONS:

1. Preheat the griddle to medium-low heat
2. Whisk eggs in a bowl with pepper and salt. Stir in basil.
3. Spray griddle top with cooking spray.
4. Add tomatoes on hot griddle top and sauté for few minutes.
5. Pour egg mixture on top of tomatoes and wait until eggs are slightly firm.
6. Add mozzarella cheese slices on top and let the omelet set.
7. Serve and enjoy.

NUTRITIONAL: Value (Amount per Serving): Calories 515 Fat 40 g Carbohydrates 5.2 g Sugar 2.1 g Protein 37 g Cholesterol 529 mg

Pumpkin Pancake

Preparation Time: 10 minutes
Cooking Time: 10 minutes
Serve: 4

Ingredients:

- 4 eggs
- 1/2 tsp cinnamon
- 1/2 cup pumpkin puree
- 1 cup almond flour
- 2 tsp liquid stevia
- 1 tsp baking powder

DIRECTIONS:

1. Preheat the griddle to medium-low heat.
2. In a bowl, mix almond flour, stevia, baking powder, cinnamon, pumpkin puree, and eggs until well combined.
3. Spray griddle top with cooking spray.
4. Drop batter onto the hot griddle top.
5. Cook pancakes until lightly golden brown from both sides.
6. Serve and enjoy.

NUTRITIONAL Value (Amount per Serving): Calories 235 Fat 18.5 g Carbohydrates 9.6 g Sugar 2.4 g Protein 11.9 g Cholesterol 164 mg

Easy Cheese Omelet

Preparation Time: 10 minutes
Cooking Time: 10 minutes
Serve: 2

INGREDIENTS:

- 6 eggs
- 7 oz cheddar cheese, shredded
- 3 oz butter
- Pepper
- Salt

DIRECTIONS:

1. In a bowl, whisk together eggs, half cheese, pepper, and salt.
2. Preheat the griddle to medium heat.
3. Melt butter on the hot griddle top.
4. Once butter is melted then pour egg mixture onto the griddle top and cook until set.
5. Add remaining cheese fold and serve.

NUTRITIONAL: Value (Amount per Serving): Calories 892 Fat 80 g Carbohydrates 2.4 g Sugar 1.6 g Protein 41.7 g Cholesterol 687 mg

Spinach Pancakes

Preparation Time: 10 minutes
Cooking Time: 10 minutes
Serve: 6

INGREDIENTS:

- 4 eggs
- 1 cup coconut milk
- 1/4 cup chia seeds
- 1 cup spinach, chopped
- 1/2 tsp black pepper
- 1/2 tsp ground nutmeg
- 1 tsp baking soda
- 1/2 cup coconut flour
- 1/2 tsp salt

DIRECTIONS:

1. In a bowl, whisk eggs with coconut milk until frothy.
2. Mix together all dry ingredients and add in the egg mixture and whisk until smooth.
3. Add spinach and stir well.
4. Preheat the griddle to medium-low heat.
5. Spray griddle top with cooking spray.
6. Pour 3-4 tablespoons of batter onto the hot griddle top and make a round pancake.
7. Cook pancake until lightly golden brown from both sides.
8. Serve and enjoy.

NUTRITIONAL: Value (Amount per Serving): Calories 111 Fat 7 g Carbohydrates 5 g Sugar 0.4 g Protein 6.3 g Cholesterol 109 mg

Spicy Egg Scrambled

Preparation Time: 10 minutes
Cooking Time: 10 minutes
Serve: 2

INGREDIENTS:

- 4 eggs
- 2 tbsp cilantro, chopped
- 1/3 cup heavy cream
- 1 tomato, diced
- 3 tbsp butter
- 1 Serrano chili pepper, chopped
- 2 tbsp scallions, sliced
- 1/4 tsp pepper
- 1/2 tsp salt

DIRECTIONS:

1. Preheat the griddle to medium heat.
2. Melt butter on top of the hot griddle.
3. Add tomato and chili pepper and sauté for 2 minutes.
4. In a bowl, whisk eggs with cilantro, cream, pepper, and salt.
5. Pour egg mixture over tomato and chili pepper and stir until egg is set.
6. Garnish with scallions and serve.

NUTRITIONAL: Value (Amount per Serving): Calories 355 Fat 33 g Carbohydrates 3 g Sugar 1.7 g Protein 12 g Cholesterol 401 mg

Chocolate Pancake

Preparation Time: 10 minutes
Cooking Time: 10 minutes
Serve: 4

INGREDIENTS:

- 2 eggs
- 1/2 tsp baking powder
- 2 tbsp erythritol
- 1 1/2 tbsp cocoa powder
- 1/4 cup ground flaxseed
- 2 tbsp water
- 1 tsp nutmeg
- 1 tsp cinnamon
- 1/4 tsp salt

DIRECTIONS:

1. In a bowl, mix ground flaxseed, baking powder, erythritol, cocoa powder, spices, and salt.
2. Add eggs and stir well.
3. Add water and stir until batter is well combined.
4. Preheat the griddle to medium-low heat.
5. Spray griddle top with cooking spray.
6. Pour a large spoonful of batter on a hot griddle top and make a pancake.
7. Cook pancake for 3-4 minutes on each side.
8. Serve and enjoy.

NUTRITIONAL: Value (Amount per Serving): Calories 138 Fat 12 g Carbohydrates 11 g Sugar 8 g Protein 4.5 g Cholesterol 82 mg

Broccoli Omelet

Preparation Time: 10 minutes
Cooking Time: 10 minutes
Serve: 2

INGREDIENTS:

- 4 eggs
- 1 cup broccoli, chopped and cooked
- 1 tbsp olive oil
- 1/4 tsp pepper
- 1/2 tsp salt

DIRECTIONS:

1. In a bowl, beat eggs with pepper, and salt.
2. Preheat the griddle to medium heat. Add oil to the griddle top.
3. Pour broccoli and egg mixture onto the hot griddle top and cook until set. Flip omelet and cook until lightly golden brown.
4. Serve and enjoy.

NUTRITIONAL: Value (Amount per Serving): Calories 203 Fat 16 g Carbohydrates 4 g Sugar 1.5 g Protein 12 g Cholesterol 327 mg

Healthy Oatmeal Pancake

Preparation Time: 10 minutes
Cooking Time: 10 minutes
Serve: 2

INGREDIENTS:

- 6 egg whites
- 1 cup steel-cut oats
- 1/4 tsp vanilla
- 1 cup Greek yogurt
- 1/2 tsp baking powder
- 1 tsp liquid stevia
- 1/4 tsp cinnamon

DIRECTIONS:

1. Preheat the griddle to medium-low heat.
2. Add oats to a blender and blend until a fine powder is a form.
3. Add remaining ingredients into the blender and blend until well combined.
4. Spray griddle top with cooking spray.
5. Pour 1/4 cup batter onto the hot griddle top.
6. Cook pancake until golden brown from both sides.
7. Serve and enjoy.

NUTRITIONAL: Value (Amount per Serving): Calories 295 Fat 4 g Carbohydrates 37 g Sugar 9 g Protein 23 g Cholesterol 7 mg

BREAKFAST SANDWICHES & BREADS

Tangy Chicken Sandwiches

Preparation time: 30 minutes
Cooking Time: 20 Minutes
Servings: 4

INGREDIENTS:

- 2 lbs. chicken breast, sliced into 4 cutlets
- potato buns, toasted
- For the marinade:
- 1/2 cup pickle juice
- tablespoon Dijon mustard
- 1 teaspoon paprika
- 1/2 teaspoon black pepper
- 1/2 teaspoon salt

DIRECTIONS:

1. Mix marinade ingredients together in a mixing bowl.
2. Place chicken in marinade and marinate for 30 minutes in the refrigerator.
3. Preheat griddle to medium-high. Wipe off extra marinade and sear chicken for 7 minutes per side, or until a meat thermometer reaches 165°F.
4. Allow chicken to rest for 5 minutes after griddling and serve on toasted buns.

NUTRITION: Calories: 2 65, Sodium: 6 85 mg, Dietary Fiber: 0.6 g, Fat: 6g, Carbs: 1 .1g, Protein: 48.4g.

Savory Chicken Burgers

If you're looking for a great alternative to traditional beef burgers, these chicken burgers are lighter and packed with flavor.

Servings: 3

Preparation time: time: 10 minutes

Cooking TIME: 20 minutes

INGREDIENTS:

- 1 lb. ground chicken
- 1/2 red onion, finely chopped
- 1 teaspoon garlic powder
- 1/2 teaspoon onion powder
- 1/4 teaspoon black pepper
- 1/2 teaspoon salt
- 3 tablespoons vegetable oil
- 3 potato buns, toasted

DIRECTIONS:

1. In a large bowl, combine the ground chicken, onion, garlic powder, onion powder, pepper, and salt. Mix well to combine. Form the chicken mixture into three equal patties. Don't work the mixture too much or the burgers will be too dense.

2. Heat your griddle to medium-high heat. Add the vegetable oil.

3. When the oil is shimmering, add the chicken patties and cook 5 minutes per side, or until the patties reach 165°F.

4. Remove the patties from the griddle and allow to rest for five minutes before serving on the toasted buns.

NUTRITION: Calories: 420, Sodium: 519 mg, Dietary Fiber: 0.6 g, Fat: 24.8g, Carbs: 2.8g, Protein: 44.2g.

Sun-Dried Tomato and Chicken Flatbreads

Preparation time: time: 5 minutes
Cooking Time: 7 minutes
Servings: 4

INGREDIENTS:

- flat breads or thin pita bread
- For the topping:
- 1⁄2 cups of sliced Griddle chicken, pre-cooked or leftovers
- 1⁄2 cup sun-dried tomatoes, coarsely chopped
- leaves fresh basil, coarsely chopped
- cups mozzarella cheese, shredded
- 1 teaspoon salt
- 1 teaspoon ground black pepper
- 1 teaspoon red pepper flakes
- Olive or chili oil, for serving

DIRECTIONS:

1. Preheat the griddle to low heat.
2. Mix all the topping ingredients together in a large mixing bowl with a rubber spatula.
3. Lay flatbreads on griddle, and top with an even amount of topping mixture; spreading to the edges of each.
4. Tent the flatbreads with foil for 5 minutes each, or until cheese is just melted.
5. Place flatbreads on a flat surface or cutting board, and cut each with a pizza cutter or kitchen scissors.
6. Drizzle with olive or chili oil to serve!

NUTRITION: Calories: 276, Sodium: 1061 mg, Dietary Fiber: 1.9g Fat: 5.7g, Carbs: 35.7g Protein: 19.8g

Turkey Pesto Panini

Preparation time: time: 5 minutes

Cooking Time: 6 minutes

Servings: 2

INGREDIENTS:

- tablespoon olive oil
- slices French bread
- 1/2 cup pesto sauce
- slices mozzarella cheese
- cups chopped leftover turkey
- 1 Roma tomato, thinly sliced
- 1 avocado, halved, seeded, peeled and sliced

Directions:

1. Preheat griddle to medium-high heat.
2. Brush each slice of bread with olive oil on one side.
3. Place 2 slices olive oil side down on the griddle.
4. Spread 2 tablespoons pesto over 1 side of French bread.
5. Top with one slice mozzarella, turkey, tomatoes, avocado, a second slice of mozzarella, and top with second half of bread to make a sandwich; repeat with remaining slices of bread.
6. Cook until the bread is golden and the cheese is melted, about 2-3 minutes per side.
7. Serve warm with your favorite salad or soup.

NUTRITION: Calories: 1129, Sodium: 1243 mg, Dietary Fiber: 10g, Fat: 70.9g, Carbs: 53.2g Protein: 73g

Classic American Burger

Preparation time: time: 15 minutes
Cooking Time: 35 minutes
Servings: 6

INGREDIENTS:

- 2 lbs. ground beef, at least 20% fat
- kosher salt
- black pepper
o tomato, sliced
- 1 yellow or red onion, sliced
- 1 head iceberg lettuce, cut into flats
- thick pieces of American or medium cheddar cheese
- seeded buns or potato buns, toasted

DIRECTIONS:

1. Divide the ground beef into 6 equals loosely formed balls. Press the balls on a flat surface to make patties. Do not over work them.
2. Generously season the patties with salt and black pepper.
3. Heat your griddle to medium-high heat.
4. Place the patties on the griddle and press down to ensure that the surface makes contact. Cook for three to four minutes.
5. Flip the patties and top with cheese. Cook an additional three to four minutes. The cheese should melt by then.
6. Remove the burgers from the griddle and place them on the buns. Top with lettuce, tomato, and onion, as well as your favorite condiments.

NUTRITION: Calories: 410, Sodium: 305 mg, Dietary Fiber: 0.9g, Fat: 18.8g, Carbs: 4.1g Protein: 53.4g

Layered Beef & Corn Burger

Preparation time: time: 20 minutes
Cooking Time: 30 minutes
Servings: 6

INGREDIENTS:

- large egg, lightly beaten
- 1 cup whole kernel corn, cooked
- 1/2 cup bread crumbs
- tablespoons shallots, minced
- 1 teaspoon Worcestershire sauce
- pounds ground beef
- 1 teaspoon salt
- 1/2 teaspoon pepper
- 1/2 teaspoon ground sage

DIRECTIONS:

1. Combine the egg, corn, bread crumbs, shallots, and Worcestershire sauce in a mixing bowl and set aside.
2. Combine ground beef and seasonings in a separate bowl.
3. Line a flat surface with waxed paper.
4. Roll beef mixture into 12 thin burger patties.
5. Spoon corn mixture into the center of 6 patties and spread evenly across within an inch of the edge.
6. Top each with a second circle of meat and press edges to seal corn mixture in the middle of each burger.
7. Griddle over medium heat, for 12-15 minutes on each side or until thermometer reads 160°F and juices run clear.

NUTRITION: Calories: 354, Sodium: 578 mg, Dietary Fiber: 1.2g Fat: 11.1g, Carbs: 12.3g Protein: 49.1g

Pork Tenderloin Sandwiches

Preparation time: time: 10 minutes
Cooking Time: 25 minutes
Servings: 6

INGREDIENTS:

- 2 (3/4-lb.) pork tenderloins
- teaspoon garlic powder
- 1 teaspoon sea salt
- 1 teaspoon dry mustard
- 1/2 teaspoon coarsely ground pepper
- Olive oil, for brushing
- whole wheat hamburger buns
- tablespoons barbecue sauce

DIRECTIONS:

1. Stir the garlic, salt, pepper, and mustard together in a small mixing bowl.
2. Rub pork tenderloins evenly with olive oil, then seasoning mix.
3. Preheat griddle to medium-high heat, and cook 10 to 12 minutes on each side or until a meat thermometer inserted into thickest portion registers 155°F.
4. Remove from griddle and let stand 10 minutes.
5. Slice thinly, and evenly distribute onto hamburger buns.
6. Drizzle each sandwich with barbecue sauce and serve.

NUTRITION: Calories: 372, Sodium: 694 mg, Dietary Fiber: 2.9g, Fat: 13.4g, Carbs: 24.7g Protein: 37.2g

Cheesy Ham and Pineapple Sandwich

Preparation time: time: 10 minutes
Cooking Time: 20 minutes
Servings: 4

INGREDIENTS:

- (10 ounce) package deli sliced ham
- pineapple rings
- slices swiss cheese
- 8 slices of thick bread
- Butter, softened, for brushing

DIRECTIONS:

1. Butter one side of all the slices of bread and heat your griddle to medium heat.
2. On top of each piece of bread, stack 1/4 of the ham, a pineapple ring, and 1 slice of cheese.
3. Place the sandwiches on the griddle and top with another slice of bread.
4. Cook until the bottom bread is golden brown, then flip and cook until the other side of the bread is browned and the cheese is melted.

NUTRITION: Calories: 594, Sodium: 3184 mg, Dietary Fiber: 0.3g, Fat: 40.3g, Carbs: 4.7g Protein: 47.7g

Croque Madame

Preparation time: time: 10 minutes

Cooking Time: 10 minutes

Servings: 2

INGREDIENTS:

- tablespoons butter
- tablespoon flour
- 2/3 cup milk
- slices thick cut bread
- slices black forest ham
- slices gruyere cheese
- Salt and black pepper
- eggs

DIRECTIONS:

1. In a small saucepan over medium heat, melt one tablespoon of butter and add the flour. Whisk until just browned and add the milk. Stir until the sauce has thickened. Remove from heat and season with salt and pepper.

2. Heat your griddle to medium heat. Butter one side of each slice of bread and add a generous amount of the bechamel sauce to the other side.

3. Place two slices of ham on top of each sandwich and top with the other slice of bread. Place on the griddle and cook until golden brown. Flip the sandwiches and top with the gruyere cheese. On the other side of the griddle, crack the eggs and cook until the whites are firm.

4. Cook until the other side of the sandwich is golden brown and the gruyere has melted on top. Top each sandwich with a fried egg before serving.

NUTRITION: Calories: 538, Sodium: 1019 mg, Dietary Fiber: 2.4g Fat: 35.2g, Carbs: 17.8g Protein: 36.9g

Salmon Burgers

Preparation time: time: 10 minutes
Cooking Time: 15 minutes
Servings: 4

INGREDIENTS:

- potato buns
- 2 lbs. salmon, finely chopped
- 1/2 red onion, finely chopped
- stalk celery, finely chopped
- 1/2 teaspoon garlic powder
- teaspoons Dijon mustard
- teaspoon salt
- slices tomato
- tablespoons vegetable oil

DIRECTIONS:

1. In a large bowl, combine the chopped salmon, onion, celery, garlic powder, mustard, and salt. Mix well and form into 4 equal patties.
2. Heat your griddle to medium heat and add the vegetable oil. When oil is shimmering add the salmon patties, cooking 6 to 7 minutes per side. Remove from the griddle, place on the buns and top with sliced tomato to serve.

NUTRITION: Calories: 512, Sodium: 935 mg, Dietary Fiber: 3.7g Fat: 22.5g, Carbs: 32.4g Protein: 49.5g

Ultimate Griddle Cheese

Preparation time: time: 10 minutes
Cooking Time: 10 minutes
Servings: 4

INGREDIENTS:

- 8 slices sourdough bread
- slices provolone cheese
- slices yellow American cheese
- 4 slices sharp cheddar cheese
- 4 slices tomato
- 3 tablespoons mayonnaise
- 3 tablespoons butter

DIRECTIONS:

1. Heat your griddle to medium heat.
2. Butter one side of each piece of bread and spread mayo on the other side.
3. Place the buttered side down on the griddle and stack the cheeses on top.
4. Place the other pieces of bread, butter side up on top of the cheese and cook until golden brown. Flip and cook until the other piece of bread is golden brown as well and the cheese is melted.
5. Remove from the griddle, slice in half and enjoy.

NUTRITION: Calories: 521, Sodium: 1044 mg, Dietary Fiber: 1.7g Fat: 30.1g, Carbs: 41.4g Protein: 22g

Garlic Parmesan Griddle Cheese Sandwiches

Preparation time: 2 minutes

Cooking Time: 7 minutes

Servings: 1

INGREDIENTS:

- 2 slices Italian bread, sliced thin
- 2 slices provolone cheese
- 2 tablespoons butter, softened
- Garlic powder, for dusting
- Dried parsley, for dusting
- Parmesan Cheese, shredded, for dusting

DIRECTIONS:

1. Spread butter evenly across 2 slices of bread and sprinkle each buttered side with garlic and parsley.

2. Sprinkle a few tablespoons of Parmesan cheese over each buttered side of bread and gently press the cheese into the bread.

3. Preheat the griddle to medium heat and place one slice of bread, buttered side down, into the griddle.

4. Top with provolone slices and second slice of bread with the butter side up.

5. Cook 3 minutes, and flip to cook 3 minutes on the other side; cook until bread is golden and parmesan cheese is crispy.

6. Serve warm with your favorite sides!

NUTRITION: Calories: 575, Sodium: 1065 mg, Dietary Fiber: 2.8g, Fat: 45.1g, Carbs: 18.1g Protein: 27.6g

Griddle Pizza Cheese

Preparation time: 10 minutes
Cooking Time: 20 minutes
Servings: 4

INGREDIENTS:

- 8 slices French bread
- 3 tablespoons butter, softened
- 1/2 cup pizza sauce
- 1/4 cup mozzarella cheese
- 1/2 cup pepperoni diced
- Garlic powder, for dusting
- Oregano, for dusting

DIRECTIONS:

1. Spread butter on one side of each French bread slice.
2. Place butter side down on a piece of aluminum foil and dust with garlic powder and oregano.
3. Spread pizza sauce on opposite side of all French bread slices.
4. Top 4 slices of bread with mozzarella cheese, a few slices of pepperoni, and additional mozzarella.
5. Place remaining French bread slices on top of pizza topped bread, butter side up, to create 4 sandwiches.
6. Preheat the griddle to medium heat and place one slice of bread, buttered side down into the griddle.
7. Cook, 3 minutes and flip to cook 3 minutes on the other side; cook until bread is golden and cheese is melted.
8. Serve warm and enjoy!

Nutrition: Calories: 305, Sodium: 664 mg, Dietary Fiber: 2.3g, Fat: 12g, Carbs: 40.4g Protein: 9.4g

Mini Portobello Burgers

Preparation time: 15 minutes
Cooking Time: 15 minutes
Servings: 4

INGREDIENTS:

- portobello mushroom caps
- slices mozzarella cheese
- 4 buns, like brioche
- For the marinade:
- 1/4 cup balsamic vinegar
- 2 tablespoons olive oil
- teaspoon dried basil
- 1 teaspoon dried oregano
- 1 teaspoon garlic powder
- ¼ teaspoon sea salt
- ¼ teaspoon black pepper

DIRECTIONS:

1. Whisk together marinade ingredients in a large mixing bowl. Add mushroom caps and toss to coat.
2. Let stand at room temperature for 15 minutes, turning twice.
3. Preheat griddle for medium-high heat.
4. Place mushrooms on the griddle; reserve marinade for basting.
5. Cook for 5 to 8 minutes on each side, or until tender.
6. Brush with marinade frequently.
7. Top with mozzarella cheese during the last 2 minutes of cooking.
8. Remove from griddle and serve on brioche buns.

NUTRITION: Calories: 248, Sodium: 429 mg, Dietary Fiber: 2.1g Fat: 13.5g, Carbs: 20.3g Protein: 13g

Veggie Pesto Flatbread

Preparation time: time: 40 minutes
Cooking Time: 10 minutes
Servings: 4

INGREDIENTS:

* 2 flatbreads
* jar pesto
* cup shredded mozzarella cheese
* For the topping:
* 1/2 cup cherry tomatoes, halved
* 1 small red onion, sliced thin
* 1 red bell pepper, sliced
* 1 yellow bell pepper, sliced
* 1/2 cup mixed black and green olives, halved
* 1 small yellow squash or zucchini, sliced
* teaspoon olive oil
* ¼ teaspoon sea salt
* ¼ teaspoon black pepper

DIRECTIONS:

1. Preheat the griddle to low heat.
2. Spread an even amount of pesto onto each flatbread.
3. Top with ½ cup mozzarella cheese each.
4. Mix all the topping ingredients together in a large mixing bowl with a rubber spatula.
5. Lay flatbreads on griddle, and top with an even amount of topping mixture; spreading to the edges of each.
6. Tent the flatbreads with foil for 5 minutes each, or until cheese is just melted.
7. Place flatbreads on a flat surface or cutting board, and cut each with a pizza cutter or kitchen scissors.
8. Serve warm!

NUTRITION: Calories: 177 Sodium: 482 mg, Dietary Fiber: 1.7g Fat: 11.9g, Carbs: 12.6g Protein: 5.5g

Griddle Vegetable Pizza

Preparation time: 30 minutes
Cooking Time: 10 minutes
Servings: 6

INGREDIENTS:

- 8 small fresh mushrooms, halved
- small zucchini, cut into 1/4-inch slices
- small yellow pepper, sliced
- 1 small red pepper, sliced
- 1 small red onion, sliced
- 1 tablespoon white wine vinegar
- 1 tablespoon water
- teaspoons olive oil, divided
- 1/2 teaspoon dried basil
- 1/4 teaspoon sea salt
- 1/4 teaspoon pepper
- 1 prebaked, 12-inch thin whole wheat pizza crust
- 1 can (8 ounces) pizza sauce
- small tomatoes, chopped
- cups shredded part-skim mozzarella cheese

DIRECTIONS:

1. Preheat your griddle to medium-high heat.
2. Combine mushrooms, zucchini, peppers, onion, vinegar, water, 3 teaspoons oil and seasonings in a large mixing bowl.
3. Transfer to griddle and cook over medium heat for 10 minutes or until tender, stirring often.
4. Brush crust with remaining oil and spread with pizza sauce.
5. Top evenly with Griddle vegetables, tomatoes and cheese.
6. Tent with aluminum foil and griddle over medium heat for 5 to 7 minutes or until edges are lightly browned and cheese is melted.
7. Serve warm!

NUTRITION: Calories: 111, Sodium: 257 mg, Dietary Fiber: 1.7g Fat: 5.4g, Carbs: 12.2g Protein: 5g

Bacon Jalapeno Wraps

Preparation time: 5 minutes
Cooking Time: 10 minutes
Servings: 4

INGREDIENTS:

- package bacon, uncured and nitrate free
- fresh jalapeno peppers, halved lengthwise and seeded
- 1 (8 ounce) package cream cheese
- 1 dozen toothpicks, soaked

DIRECTIONS:

1. Preheat your griddle to high heat.
2. Fill jalapeno halves with cream cheese.
3. Wrap each with bacon. Secure with a toothpick.
4. Place on the griddle, and cook until bacon is crispy, about 5 to 7 minutes per side.
5. Remove to a platter to cool and serve warm.

NUTRITION: Calories: 379, Sodium: 1453 mg, Dietary Fiber: 0.9g Fat: 33.4g, Carbs: 3.5g Protein: 16.3g

MAIN DISHES: PORK

Pork Tenderloin Sandwiches

Tender Griddle pork is the perfect way to griddle up a savory sandwich on your outdoor griddle. This simple, yet flavorful sandwich will have you griddling like a gourmet chef in no time.

Servings: 6 **Preparation time:** 10 minutes | **Cooking time:** 25 minutes

INGREDIENTS:

- 2 (3/4-lb.) pork tenderloins
- 1 teaspoon garlic powder
- 1 teaspoon sea salt
- 1 teaspoon dry mustard
- 1/2 teaspoon coarsely ground pepper
- Olive oil, for brushing
- 6 whole wheat hamburger buns
- 6 tablespoons barbecue sauce

DIRECTIONS:

1. Stir the garlic, salt, pepper, and mustard together in a small mixing bowl.
2. Rub pork tenderloins evenly with olive oil, then seasoning mix.
3. Preheat griddle to medium-high heat, and cook 10 to 12 minutes on each side or until a meat thermometer inserted into thickest portion registers 155°F.
4. Remove from griddle and let stand 10 minutes.
5. Slice thinly, and evenly distribute onto hamburger buns.
6. Drizzle each sandwich with barbecue sauce and serve.

NUTRITION: Calories: 372, Sodium: 694mg, Dietary Fiber: 2.9g, Fat: 13.4g, Carbs: 24.7g, Protein: 37.2g.

Herb-Crusted Mediterranean Pork Tenderloin

Herb-Crusted Tenderloin with Mediterranean style spices is one great way to griddle up juicy tenderloin. My favorite way to serve this dish is alongside lemon chili pasta and salad with a glass of Pinot Grigio.

Servings: 4 | **Preparation time:** time: 2 hours | **Cooking TIME:** 30 minutes

INGREDIENTS:

- 1-pound pork tenderloin
- 1 tablespoon olive oil
- 2 teaspoons dried oregano
- 3/4 teaspoon lemon pepper
- 1 teaspoon garlic powder
- 1/4 cup parmesan cheese, grated
- 3 tablespoons olive tapenade

DIRECTIONS:

1. Place pork on a large piece of plastic wrap.
2. Rub tenderloin with oil, and sprinkle oregano, garlic powder, and lemon pepper evenly over entire tenderloin.
3. Wrap tightly in the plastic wrap and refrigerate for 2 hours.
4. Preheat griddle to medium-high heat.
5. Transfer pork to cutting board, remove plastic wrap, and make a lengthwise cut through center of tenderloin, opening meat so it lies flat, but do not cut all the way through.
6. Combine tapenade and parmesan in a small mixing bowl; rub into the center of the tenderloin and fold meat back together.
7. Tie together with twine in 2-inch intervals.
8. Sear tenderloin for 20 minutes, turning tenderloin once during griddling, or until internal temperature reaches 145°F.
9. Transfer tenderloin to cutting board.
10. Tent with foil; let rest for 10 minutes.
11. Remove string and cut into 1/4-inch-thick slices and serve.

NUTRITION: Calories: 413, Sodium: 1279mg, Dietary Fiber: 0.5g, Fat: 30.5g, Carbs: 2.4g, Protein: 31.4g.

Paprika Dijon Pork Tenderloin

This tender pork loin is paired perfectly with the earthy flavor of mustard for a dish that is sure to please guests or you family. The addition of a little smoked paprika compliments the robust mustard and delicate pork tenderloin.

Servings: 6 | **Preparation time:** time: 10 minutes | **Cooking TIME:** 4 hours

INGREDIENTS:

- 2 1 lb. pork tenderloins
- 2 tablespoons Dijon mustard
- 1-1/2 teaspoons smoked paprika
- 1 teaspoon salt
- 2 tablespoons olive oil

DIRECTIONS:

1. In a small bowl, combine the mustard and paprika.
2. Set your griddle to medium heat.
3. Rub the tenderloins with the mustard mixture, making sure they are evenly coated.
4. Place the tenderloins on the griddle and cook until all sides are well browned, and the internal temperature is 135°F.
5. Remove the tenderloins from the griddle and rest 5 minutes before slicing and serving.

NUTRITION: Calories: 484, Sodium: 755mg, Dietary Fiber: 4.2g, Fat: 24.7g, Carbs: 13.8g, Protein: 50.9g.

Moroccan Spiced Pork Tenderloin with Creamy Harissa Sauce

Moroccan spice and creamy harissa make for one delicious way to serve up tender pork any night of the week. Enjoy this yummy dish with collard greens and potato salad for a taste twist on your next cookout.

Servings: 6 | **Preparation time:** time: 40 minutes | **Cooking TIME:** 20 minutes

INGREDIENTS:

- 2 (1 lb.) pork tenderloins
- 1 teaspoon ground cinnamon
- 1 teaspoon ground cilantro
- 1 teaspoon ground cumin
- 1 teaspoon paprika
- 1 teaspoon sea salt
- 2 tablespoons olive oil
- For Creamy Harissa Sauce:
- 1 cup Greek yogurt (8 ounces)
- 1 tablespoon fresh lemon juice
- 1 tablespoon extra-virgin olive oil
- 1 teaspoon harissa sauce
- 1 clove garlic, minced
- Kosher salt and cracked black pepper

DIRECTIONS:

1. Combine harissa ingredients in a small mixing bowl and set aside.
2. Combine the cinnamon, coriander, cumin, paprika, salt and olive oil.
3. Rub the seasonings evenly over the pork tenderloins; cover and refrigerate for 30 minutes.
4. Preheat griddle to high heat and cook tenderloins until browned; about 8 to 10 minutes.
5. Turn and cook an additional 8 to 10 minutes. Transfer the tenderloins to a cutting board, tent with foil and rest for 10 minutes.
6. Slice and serve with creamy harissa sauce.

NUTRITION: Calories: 376, Sodium: 458mg, Dietary Fiber: 0.4g, Fat: 17.9g, Carbs: 2.6g, Protein: 48.7g.

Sticky-Sweet Pork Shoulder

Sweet and sticky sauce is the perfect complement to savory Griddle pork. Serve this delicious dish with your favorite sides or as a delicious stuffing for steamed buns or Griddle bread.

Servings: 6 – 8 | **Preparation time:** time: 8 hours | **Cooking TIME:** 8 minutes

INGREDIENTS:

- 1 (5 lbs.) Boston Butt pork shoulder
- For the marinade:
- 2 tablespoons garlic, minced
- 1 large piece ginger, peeled and chopped
- 1 cup hoisin sauce
- 3/4 cup fish sauce
- 2/3 cup honey
- 2/3 cup Shaoxing
- 1/2 cup chili oil
- 1/3 cup oyster sauce
- 1/3 cup sesame oil
- For the glaze:
- 3/4 cup dark brown sugar
- 1 tablespoon light molasses

DIRECTIONS:

1. Place pork shoulder, fat side down, on a cutting board with a short end facing you. Holding a long sharp knife about 1"–1½" above cutting board, make a shallow cut along the entire length of a long side of shoulder.
2. Continue cutting deeper into meat, lifting and unfurling with your free hand, until it lies flat.
3. Purée marinade in a blender and reserve 1 ½ cups for glaze, cover and refrigerate.
4. Pour remaining marinade in a large sealable plastic bag.
5. Add pork shoulder to bag and marinate in the refrigerator for 8 hours.
6. Preheat griddle to medium heat (with cover closed, thermometer should register 350°). Remove pork from marinade, letting excess drip off.
7. Add glaze ingredients to reserved marinade until sugar is dissolved.
8. Griddle pork, for 8 minutes, basting and turning with tongs every minute or so, until thick coated with glaze, lightly charred in spots, and warmed through; an instant-read thermometer inserted into the thickest part should register 145°F.
9. Transfer to a cutting board and slice against the grain, ¼" thick, to serve.

NUTRITION: Calories: 1286, Sodium: 2875mg, Dietary Fiber: 1g, Fat: 84.8g, Carbs: 58.3g, Protein: 68.7g.

Griddle Pork Chops with Herb Apple Compote

Apples are one of my absolute favorite ingredients to pair with pork chops, and I hope you love this recipe too! Sweet meets juicy pork for a griddling flavor that is out of this world.

Servings: 4 | **Preparation time:** time: 5 minutes | **Cooking TIME:** 20 minutes

INGREDIENTS:

- 4, bone-in pork chops
- 2 honey crisp apples, peeled, cored and chopped
- 1/3 cup orange juice
- 1 teaspoon chopped fresh rosemary
- 1 teaspoon chopped fresh sage
- Sea salt
- Black pepper

DIRECTIONS:

1. Add the apples, herbs and orange juice to a saucepan and simmer over medium heat until the apples are tender and the juices are thickened to a thin syrup, about 10 to 12 minutes.
2. Season pork chops with salt and pepper.
3. Place on the griddle and cook until the pork chop releases from the griddle, about 4 minutes.
4. Flip and cook on the other side for 3 minutes.
5. Transfer to a cutting board and tent with foil.
6. Top with apple compote and serve!

NUTRITION: Calories: 284, Sodium: 173mg, Dietary Fiber: 1g, Fat: 20g, Carbs: 7.2g, Protein: 18.2g.

Yucatan-Style Griddle Pork

Elevate simple Griddle pork with Yucatan citrus combinations to make something different on your outdoor griddle Serve this with a side of Griddle plantains, veggies, and sparkling water.

Servings: 4 | **Preparation time:** time: 15 minutes | **Cooking time:** 8 minutes

INGREDIENTS:

- 2 pork tenderloins, trimmed
- 1 teaspoon annatto powder
- Olive oil
- For the marinade:
- 2 oranges, juiced
- 2 lemons, juiced, or more to taste
- 2 limes, juiced, or more to taste
- 6 cloves garlic, minced
- 1 teaspoon ground cumin
- 1/2 teaspoon cayenne pepper
- 1/2 teaspoon dried oregano
- 1/2 teaspoon black pepper

DIRECTIONS:

1. Combine marinade ingredients in a mixing bowl and whisk until well-blended.
2. Cut the tenderloins in half crosswise; cut each piece in half lengthwise.
3. Place pieces in marinade and thoroughly coat with the mixture.
4. Cover with plastic wrap and refrigerate 4 to 6 hours.
5. Transfer pieces of pork from marinade to a paper-towel-lined bowl to absorb most of the moisture.
6. Discard paper towels. Drizzle olive oil and a bit more annatto powder on the pork.
7. Preheat griddle for medium-high heat and lightly oil.
8. Place pieces evenly spaced on griddle; cook 4 to 5 minutes.
9. Turn and cook on the other side another 4 or 5 minutes.
10. Transfer onto a serving platter and allow meat to rest about 5 minutes before serving.

NUTRITION: Calories: 439, Sodium: 1382mg, Dietary Fiber: 1.5g, Fat: 33.1g, Carbs: 11.4g, Protein: 23.9g.

Glazed Country Ribs

Country ribs are full of delicious flavor and make for one great main dish on weeknights or weekends with friends. Serve these ribs with your favorite sides and cold, crisp beer on summer holidays for traditional griddling fun.

Servings: 6 | **Preparation time:** time: 10 minutes | **Cooking TIME:** 4 hours

INGREDIENTS:

- 3 pounds country-style pork ribs
- 1 cup low-sugar ketchup
- 1/2 cup water
- 1/4 cup onion, finely chopped
- 1/4 cup cider vinegar or wine vinegar
- 1/4 cup light molasses
- 2 tablespoons Worcestershire sauce
- 2 teaspoons chili powder
- 2 cloves garlic, minced

DIRECTIONS:

1. Combine ketchup, water, onion, vinegar, molasses, Worcestershire sauce, chili powder, and garlic in a saucepan and bring to boil; reduce heat. Simmer, uncovered, for 10 to 15 minutes or until desired thickness is reached, stirring often.
2. Trim fat from ribs.
3. Preheat griddle to medium-high.
4. Place ribs, bone-side down, on griddle and cook for 1-1/2 to 2 hours or until tender, brushing occasionally with sauce during the last 10 minutes of cooking.
5. Serve with remaining sauce and enjoy!

NUTRITION: Calories: 404, Sodium: 733mg, Dietary Fiber: 0.4g, Fat: 8.1g, Carbs: 15.2g, Protein: 60.4g.

Pineapple Bacon Pork Chops

Sweet and juicy pineapple compliments savory pork for one incredible dish! You'll love the sweet and spicy kick in this recipe - serve it with your favorite Griddle side dishes and vegetables and a cold glass of beer or iced tea.

Servings: 6 | **Preparation time:** time: 30 minutes | **Cooking TIME:** 1 hour

INGREDIENTS:

- 1 large whole pineapple
- 6 pork chops
- 12 slices thick-cut bacon
- Toothpicks, soaked in water
- For the glaze:
- 1/4 cup honey
- 1/8 teaspoon cayenne pepper

DIRECTIONS:

1. Turn both burners to medium-high heat; after about 15 minutes, turn off one of the middle burners and turn the remaining burners down to medium.
2. Slice off the top and bottom of the pineapple, and peel the pineapple, cutting the skin off in strips.
3. Cut pineapple flesh into six quarters.
4. Wrap each pineapple section with a bacon slice; secure each end with a toothpick.
5. Brush quarters with honey and sprinkle with cayenne pepper.
6. Put the quarters on the griddle, flipping when bacon is cooked so that both sides are evenly Griddle.
7. While pineapple quarters are cooking, coat pork chops with honey and cayenne pepper. Set on griddle.
8. Tent with foil and cook for 20 minutes. Flip, and continue cooking an additional 10 to 20 minutes or until chops are fully cooked.
9. Serve each chop with a pineapple quarter on the side.

NUTRITION: Calories: 380, Sodium: 852mg, Dietary Fiber: 0.5g, Fat: 23.5g, Carbs: 18.2g, Protein: 25.8g.

Habanero-Marinated Pork Chops

Kick things up a notch on your outdoor griddle with this spicy recipe. These yummy pork chops pair perfectly with yellow rice, black beans, and your favorite salad.

Servings: 4 | **Preparation time:** time: 30 minutes | **Cooking TIME:** 13 minutes

INGREDIENTS:

- 4-1/2-inch-thick bone-in pork chops
- 3 tablespoons olive oil, plus more for griddle
- Kosher salt and freshly ground black pepper
- For the marinade:
- 1 habanero chili, seeded, chopped fine
- 2 garlic cloves, minced
- 1/2 cup fresh orange juice
- 2 tablespoons brown sugar
- 1 tablespoon apple cider vinegar

DIRECTIONS:

1. Combine marinade ingredients in a large sealable plastic bag.
2. Pierce pork chops all over with a fork and add to bag, seal, and turn to coat.
3. Marinate at room temperature, turning occasionally, for 30 minutes.
4. griddle for medium-high heat.
5. Brush the griddle with oil.
6. Remove pork chops from marinade and pat dry.
7. Sear for 8 minutes, turning occasionally, until charred and cooked through.
8. Transfer to a plate and let rest 5 minutes.
9. Serve with your favorite sides.

NUTRITION: Calories: 490, Sodium: 171mg, Dietary Fiber: 1.1g, Fat: 39.2g, Carbs: 10.9g, Protein: 23.3g.

Garlic Soy Pork Chops

Sweet and spicy ribs are a great way to griddle out with the whole family on the weekends. Serve these sticky ribs with mashed potatoes and Griddle vegetables for some decadent weekend backyard fun.

Servings: 4 – 6 | **Preparation time:** time: 8 hours | **Cooking TIME:** 1 hour

INGREDIENTS:

- 4 to 6 pork chops
- 4 cloves garlic, finely chopped
- 1/2 cup olive oil
- 1/2 cup soy sauce
- 1/2 teaspoon garlic powder
- 1/2 teaspoon salt
- 1/2 black pepper
- 1/4 cup butter

DIRECTIONS:

1. In a large zipper lock bag, combine the garlic, olive oil, soy sauce, and garlic powder. Add the pork chops and make sure the marinade coats the chops. Set aside for 30 minutes.
2. Heat your griddle to medium-high heat. Add 2 tablespoons of olive oil and 2 tablespoons of butter to the griddle.
3. Add the chops to the griddle one at a time, making sure they are not crowded. Add another 2 tablespoons of butter to the griddle and cook the chops for 4 minutes. Cook an additional 4 minutes.
4. Remove the chops from the griddle and spread the remaining butter over them. Serve after resting for 5 minutes.

NUTRITION: Calories: 398, Sodium: 1484mg, Dietary Fiber: 0.2g, Fat: 37.7g, Carbs: 2.5g, Protein: 13.6g.

Honey Soy Pork Chops

Sweet and tangy Griddle pork is absolutely delicious when Griddle to perfection on your outdoor griddle. Simply serve this dish with rice and Griddle vegetables for one delicious meal.

Servings: 6 | **Preparation time:** time: 1 hour | **Cooking TIME:** 25 minutes

INGREDIENTS:

- 6 (4 ounce) boneless pork chops
- 1/4 cup organic honey
- 1 to 2 tablespoons low sodium soy sauce
- 2 tablespoons olive oil
- 1 tablespoon rice mirin

DIRECTIONS:

1. Combine honey, soy sauce, oil, and white vinegar and whisk until well-combined. Add sauce and pork chops to a large sealable plastic bag and marinate for 1 hour.
2. Preheat the griddle to medium-high heat and cook for 4 to 5 minutes, or until the pork chop easily releases from the griddle.
3. Flip and continue to cook for 5 additional minutes, or until internal temperature reaches 145°F.
4. Serve and enjoy!

NUTRITION: Calories: 251, Sodium: 187mg, Dietary Fiber: 0.1g, Fat: 8.7g, Carbs: 13.1g, Protein: 29.9g.

Cuban Pork Chops

These authentic Cuban pork chops are easy to make are a packed with exotic flavors. Thanks to your outdoor griddle they are sure to cook to perfection.

Servings: 4 |**Preparation time**30 minutes |
Cooking time: 1 hour 30 minutes

INGREDIENTS:

- 4 pork chops
- 4 cloves garlic, smashed
- 2 tablespoons olive oil
- 1/3 cup lime juice
- 1/4 cup water
- 1 teaspoon ground cumin
- Salt and black pepper

DIRECTIONS:

1. Set your griddle to medium. Salt the pork chops on both side and cook the chops until lightly browned.
2. Combine the water, garlic, and lime juice in a bowl and whisk until even.
3. Continue cooking the pork chops while basting them with the lime juice mixture.
4. When the pork chops have finished cooking, remove from the griddle and top with additional sauce and black pepper before serving.

NUTRITION: Calories: 323, Sodium: 58mg, Dietary Fiber: 0.1g, Fat: 27g, Carbs: 1.5g, Protein: 18.3g.

Spicy Cajun Pork Chops

Packed with flavor and a nice amount of heat, these Cajun pork chops are perfect for outdoor cooking any time of year. For best results, serve with a nice, rich coleslaw.

Servings: 4 | **Preparation time:** time: 10 minutes | **Cooking TIME:** 15 minutes

INGREDIENTS:

- 4 pork chops
- 1 tablespoon paprika
- 1/2 teaspoon ground cumin
- 1/2 teaspoon dried sage
- 1/2 teaspoon salt
- 1/2 teaspoon black pepper
- 1/2 teaspoon garlic powder
- 1/4 teaspoon cayenne pepper
- 1 tablespoon butter
- 1 tablespoon vegetable oil

DIRECTIONS:

1. In a medium bowl, combine the paprika, cumin, sage, salt, pepper, garlic, and cayenne pepper.
2. Heat your griddle to medium-high heat and add the butter and oil.
3. Rub the pork chops with a generous amount of the seasoning rub.
4. Place the chops on the griddle and cook for 4 to 5 minutes. Turn the pork chops and continue cooking an additional 4 minutes.
5. Remove the pork chops from the griddle and allow to rest 5 minutes before serving.

NUTRITION: Calories: 320, Sodium: 368mg, Dietary Fiber: 0.8g, Fat: 26.5g, Carbs: 1.6g, Protein: 18.4g.

MAIN DISHES: POULTRY

Classic BBQ Chicken

Preparation time: time: 5 minutes
Cooking Time: 1 hour 45 minutes
Servings: 4-6

INGREDIENTS:

- pounds of your favorite chicken, including legs, thighs, wings, and breasts, skin-on
- Salt
- Olive oil
- cup barbecue sauce, like Hickory Mesquite or homemade

DIRECTIONS:

1. Rub the chicken with olive oil and salt.
2. Preheat the griddle to high heat.
3. Sear chicken skin side down on the griddle for 5-10 minutes.
4. Turn the griddle down to medium low heat, tent with foil and cook for 30 minutes.
5. Turn chicken and baste with barbecue sauce.
6. Cover the chicken again and allow to cook for another 20 minutes.
7. Baste, cover and cook again for 30 minutes; repeat basting and turning during this time.
8. The chicken is done when the internal temperature of the chicken pieces is 165°F and juices run clear.
9. Baste with more barbecue sauce to serve!

NUTRITION: Calories: 539, Sodium: 684 mg, Dietary Fiber: 0.3 g, Fat: 11.6 g, Carbs: 15.1 g, Protein: 87.6 g.

California Seared Chicken

Preparation time: time: 35 minutes

Cooking Time: 20 minutes

Servings: 4

INGREDIENTS:

- boneless, skinless chicken breasts
- 3/4 cup balsamic vinegar
- tablespoons extra virgin olive oil
- tablespoon honey
- 1 teaspoon oregano
- 1 teaspoon basil
- 1 teaspoon garlic powder
- For garnish:
- Sea salt
- Black pepper, fresh ground
- slices fresh mozzarella cheese
- 4 slices avocado
- 4 slices beefsteak tomato
- Balsamic glaze, for drizzling

DIRECTIONS:

1. Whisk together balsamic vinegar, honey, olive oil, oregano, basil and garlic powder in a large mixing bowl.
2. Add chicken to coat and marinate for 30 minutes in the refrigerator.
3. Preheat griddle to medium-high. Sear chicken for 7 minutes per side, or until a meat thermometer reaches 165°F.
4. Top each chicken breast with mozzarella, avocado, and tomato and tent with foil on the griddle to melt for 2 minutes.
5. Garnish with a drizzle of balsamic glaze, and a pinch of sea salt and black pepper.

NUTRITION: Calories: 883, Sodium: 449 mg, Dietary Fiber: 15.2 g, Fat: 62.1 g, Carbs: 29.8 g, Protein: 55.3 g.

Sweet Chili Lime Chicken

Preparation time: time: 35 minutes
Cooking Time: 15 minutes
Servings: 4

INGREDIENTS:

- ½ cup sweet chili sauce
- ¼ cup soy sauce
- teaspoon mirin
- teaspoon orange juice, fresh squeezed
- 1 teaspoon orange marmalade
- tablespoons lime juice
- 1 tablespoon brown sugar
- 1 clove garlic, minced
- boneless, skinless chicken breasts
- Sesame seeds, for garnish

DIRECTIONS:

1. Whisk sweet chili sauce, soy sauce, mirin, orange marmalade, lime and orange juice, brown sugar, and minced garlic together in a small mixing bowl.
2. Set aside ¼ cup of the sauce.
3. Toss chicken in sauce to coat and marinate 30 minutes.
4. Preheat your griddle to medium heat.
5. Put the chicken on the griddle and cook each side for 7 minutes.
6. Baste the cooked chicken with remaining marinade and garnish with sesame seeds to serve with your favorite sides.

Nutrition: Calories: 380, Sodium: 1274 mg, Dietary Fiber: 0.5 g, Fat: 12 g, Carbs:19.7g, Protein: 43.8 g.

Seared Spicy Citrus Chicken

Preparation time: time: 8 - 24 hours
Cooking Time: 20 minutes
Servings: 4

INGREDIENTS:

- 2 lbs. boneless, skinless chicken thighs
- For the marinade:
- 1/4 cup fresh lime juice
- 2 teaspoon lime zest
- 1/4 cup honey
- 2 tablespoons olive oil
- tablespoon balsamic vinegar
- 1/2 teaspoon sea salt
- 1/2 teaspoon black pepper
- garlic cloves, minced
- 1/4 teaspoon onion powder

DIRECTIONS:

1. Whisk together marinade ingredients in a large mixing bowl; reserve 2 tablespoons of the marinade for basting.
2. Add chicken and marinade to a sealable plastic bag and marinate 8 hours or overnight in the refrigerator.
3. Preheat griddle to medium high heat and brush lightly with olive oil.
4. Place chicken on griddle and cook 8 minutes per side.
5. Baste each side of chicken with reserved marinade during the last few minutes of cooking; chicken is done when the internal temperature reaches 165°F.
6. Plate chicken, tent with foil, and allow to rest for 5 minutes.
7. Serve and enjoy!

NUTRITION: Calories: 381, Sodium: 337mg, Dietary Fiber: 1.1 g, Fat: 20.2 g, Carbs: 4.7 g, Protein: 44.7 g.

Honey Balsamic Marinated Chicken

Preparation time: time: 30 minutes - 4 hours
Cooking Time: 20 minutes
Servings: 4

INGREDIENTS:

- 2 lbs. boneless, skinless chicken thighs
- teaspoon olive oil
- 1/2 teaspoon sea salt
- 1/4 teaspoon black pepper
- 1/2 teaspoon paprika
- 3/4 teaspoon onion powder
- For the Marinade:
- tablespoons honey
- tablespoons balsamic vinegar
- 2 tablespoons tomato paste
- teaspoon garlic, minced

DIRECTIONS:

1. Add chicken, olive oil, salt, black pepper, paprika, and onion powder to a sealable plastic bag. Seal and toss to coat, covering chicken with spices and oil; set aside.
2. Whisk together balsamic vinegar, tomato paste, garlic, and honey.
3. Divide the marinade in half. Add one half to the bag of chicken and store the other half in a sealed container in the refrigerator.
4. Seal the bag and toss chicken to coat. Refrigerate for 30 minutes to 4 hours.
5. Preheat a griddle to medium-high.
6. Discard bag and marinade. Add chicken to the griddle and cook 7 minutes per side or until juices run clear and a meat thermometer reads 165°F.
7. During last minute of cooking, brush remaining marinade on top of the chicken thighs.
8. Serve immediately.

NUTRITION: Calories: 485, Sodium: 438 mg, Dietary Fiber: 0.5 g, Fat: 18.1 g, Carbs: 11 g, Protein: 66.1 g.

Salsa Verde Marinated Chicken

Preparation time: time: 4 hours 35 minutes
Cooking Time: 4 hours 50 minutes
Servings: 6

INGREDIENTS:

- boneless, skinless chicken breasts
- tablespoon olive oil
- 1 teaspoon sea salt
- 1 teaspoon chili powder
- 1 teaspoon ground cumin
- 1 teaspoon garlic powder
- For the salsa Verde marinade:
- teaspoons garlic, minced
- 1 small onion, chopped
- tomatillos, husked, rinsed and chopped
- 1 medium jalapeño pepper, cut in half, seeded
- ¼ cup fresh cilantro, chopped
- ½ teaspoon sugar or sugar substitute

DIRECTIONS:

1. Add salsa Verde marinade ingredients to a food processor and pulse until smooth.
2. Mix sea salt, chili powder, cumin, and garlic powder together in a small mixing bowl. Season chicken breasts with olive oil and seasoning mix, and lay in glass baking dish.
3. Spread a tablespoon of salsa Verde marinade over each chicken breast to cover; reserve remaining salsa for serving.
4. Cover dish with plastic wrap and refrigerate for 4 hours.
5. Preheat griddle to medium-high and brush with olive oil.
6. Add chicken to griddle and cook 7 minutes per side or until juices run clear and a meat thermometer reads 165°F.
7. Serve each with additional salsa Verde and enjoy!

NUTRITION: Calories: 321, Sodium: 444 mg, Dietary Fiber: 1.3 g, Fat: 13.7 g, Carbs: 4.8 g, Protein: 43 g.

Hasselback Stuffed Chicken

Preparation time: time: 15 minutes
Cooking Time: 30 minutes
Servings: 4

INGREDIENTS:

- boneless, skinless chicken breasts
- 2 tablespoons olive oil
- 2 tablespoons taco seasoning
- 1/2 red, yellow and green pepper, very thinly sliced
- small red onion, very thinly sliced
- 1/2 cup Mexican shredded cheese
- Guacamole, for serving
- Sour cream, for serving
- Salsa, for serving

DIRECTIONS:

1. Preheat griddle to med-high.
2. Cut thin horizontal cuts across each chicken breast; like you would Hassel back potatoes.
3. Rub chicken evenly with olive oil and taco seasoning.
4. Add a mixture of bell peppers and red onions to each cut, and place the breasts on the griddle.
5. Cook chicken for 15 minutes.
6. Remove and top with cheese.
7. Tent loosely with foil and cook another 5 minutes, until cheese is melted.
8. Remove from griddle and top with guacamole, sour cream and salsa. Serve alongside your favorite side dishes!

NUTRITION: Calories: 643, Sodium:1549 mg, Dietary Fiber: 3.8 g, Fat: 18.6g, Carbs: 26.3g, Protein: 93.3g.

Creole Chicken Stuffed with Cheese & Peppers

Preparation time: time: 10 minutes
Cooking Time: 20 minutes
Servings: 4

INGREDIENTS:

- boneless, skinless chicken breasts
- 8 mini sweet peppers, sliced thin and seeded
- 2 slices pepper jack cheese, cut in half
- 2 slices Colby jack cheese, cut in half
- tablespoon creole seasoning, like Emeril's
- 1 teaspoon black pepper
- 1 teaspoon garlic powder
- 1 teaspoon onion powder
- teaspoons olive oil, separated
- Toothpicks

DIRECTIONS:

1. Rinse chicken and pat dry.
2. Mix creole seasoning, pepper, garlic powder, and onion powder together in a small mixing bowl and set aside.
3. Cut a slit on the side of each chicken breast; be careful not to cut all the way through the chicken.
4. Rub each breast with 1 teaspoon each of olive oil.
5. Rub each chicken breast with seasoning mix and coat evenly.
6. Stuff each breast of chicken with 1 half pepper jack cheese slice, 1 half Colby cheese slice, and a handful of pepper slices.
7. Secure chicken shut with 4 or 5 toothpicks.
8. Preheat the griddle to medium-high and cook chicken for 8 minutes per side; or until chicken reaches an internal temperature of 165°F.
9. Allow chicken to rest for 5 minutes, remove toothpicks, and serve.

NUTRITION: Calories: 509, Sodium: 1117 mg, Dietary Fiber: 3.4 g, Fat: 25.1g, Carbs: 19.8g, Protein: 51.4g.

Root Beer Can Chicken

Preparation time: time: 8 hours and 10 minutes
Cooking Time: 20 minutes
Servings: 2 -4

INGREDIENTS:

- lb. boneless chicken thighs
- (12 ounce) cans root beer, like A&W
- Olive oil
- For the rub:
- tablespoon garlic powder
- 3/4 tablespoon sea salt
- 1/2 tablespoon white pepper
- teaspoons smoked paprika
- teaspoons garlic powder
- 1 teaspoon dried thyme
- 1/8 teaspoon cayenne pepper

DIRECTIONS:

1. Combine rub ingredients in a bowl; reserve half in a separate air tight container until ready to cook.
2. Rub chicken thighs evenly with olive oil and coat each with some rub.
3. Lay chicken in a 13 by 9-inch baking dish. Cover with 2 cans of root beer.
4. Preheat griddle to medium-high heat.
5. Discard marinade and brush griddle with olive oil.
6. Gently fold remaining rub and a half of the third can of root beer in a small bowl.
7. Sear chicken for 7 minutes on each side, basting often with root beer rub mix.
8. Serve when cooked through or chicken reaches 165°F and juices run clear.

NUTRITION: Calories: 363, Sodium: 1185 mg, Dietary Fiber: 0.9g, Fat: 12.1g, Carbs: 29.9g, Protein: 33.4g.

Chipotle Adobe Chicken

Preparation time: Time: 1 - 24 hours

Cooking Time: 20 minutes

Servings: 4 - 6

INGREDIENTS:

- 2 lbs. chicken thighs or breasts (boneless, skinless)
- For the marinade:
- ¼ cup olive oil
- 2 chipotle peppers, in adobo sauce, plus 1 teaspoon adobo sauce from the can
- 1 tablespoon garlic, minced
- 1 shallot, finely chopped
- 1 ½ tablespoons cumin
- 1 tablespoon cilantro, super-finely chopped or dried
- 2 teaspoons chili powder
- 1 teaspoon dried oregano
- 1/2 teaspoon salt
- Fresh limes, garnish
- Cilantro, garnish

DIRECTIONS:

1. Preheat griddle to medium-high.
2. Add marinade ingredients to a food processor or blender and pulse into a paste.
3. Add the chicken and marinade to a sealable plastic bag and massage to coat well.
4. Place in the refrigerator for 1 hour to 24 hours before cooking.
5. Sear chicken for 7 minutes, turn and cook and additional 7 minutes.
6. Turn heat to low and continue to cook until chicken has reached an internal temperature of 165°F.
7. Remove chicken from griddle and allow to rest 5 to 10 minutes before serving.
8. Garnish with a squeeze of fresh lime and a sprinkle of cilantro to serve.

NUTRITION: Calories: 561, Sodium: 431 mg, Dietary Fiber: 0.3 g, Fat: 23.8 g, Carbs: 18.7 g, Protein: 65.9 g.

Chicken Tacos with Avocado Crema

Preparation time: Time: 1 hour 5 minutes
Cooking Time: 10 minutes
Servings: 4-5

INGREDIENTS:

- 1/2 lbs. Boneless, skinless chicken breasts, sliced thin
- For the chicken marinade:
- 1 serrano pepper, minced
- teaspoons garlic, minced
- 1 lime, juiced
- 1 teaspoon ground cumin
- 1/3 cup olive oil
- Sea salt, to taste
- Black pepper, to taste
- For the avocado crema:
- 1 cup sour cream
- 2 teaspoons lime juice
- 1 teaspoon lime zest
- 1 serrano pepper, diced and seeded
- 1 clove garlic, minced
- 1 large hass avocado
- For the garnish:
- 1/2 cup queso fresco, crumbled
- 2 teaspoons cilantro, chopped
- 1 lime sliced into wedges
- 10 corn tortillas

DIRECTIONS:

1. Mix chicken marinade together in a sealable plastic bag. Add chicken and toss to coat well.
2. Marinate for 1 hour in the refrigerator.
3. Combine avocado crema ingredients in a food processor or blender and pulse until smooth.
4. Cover and refrigerate until you are ready to assemble tacos.
5. Preheat griddle to medium heat and griddle chicken for 5 minutes per side; rotating and turning as needed.
6. Remove from griddle and tent loosely with aluminum foil. Allow chicken to rest 5 minutes.
7. Serve with warm tortillas, a dollop of avocado crema, queso fresco, cilantro and lime wedges.
8. To meal Preparation time: simply divide chicken into individual portion containers with a serving of the garnish, and take with tortillas wrapped in parchment paper to warm in a microwave to serve.

NUTRITION: Calories: 703, Sodium: 357 mg, Dietary Fiber: 6.3 g, Fat: 44.5 g, Carbs: 30.5g, Protein: 47.9g.

Sizzling Chicken Fajitas

Preparation time: time: 5 minutes

Cooking Time: 25 minutes

Servings: 4

INGREDIENTS:

- boneless chicken breast halves, thinly sliced
- yellow onion, sliced
- large green bell pepper, sliced
- 1 large red bell pepper, sliced
- 1 teaspoon ground cumin
- 1 teaspoon garlic powder
- 1 teaspoon onion powder
- tablespoons lime juice
- 1 tablespoon olive oil
- 1/2 teaspoon black pepper
- 1 teaspoon salt
- tablespoons vegetable oil
- 10 flour tortillas

DIRECTIONS:

1. In a zipper lock bag, combine the chicken, cumin, garlic, onion, lime juice, salt, pepper, and olive oil. Allow to marinate for 30 minutes.
2. Preheat griddle to medium heat.
3. On one side of the griddle add the olive oil and heat until shimmering. Add the onion and pepper and cook until slightly softened.
4. On the other side of the griddle add the marinated chicken and cook until lightly browned.
5. Once chicken is lightly browned, toss together with the onion and pepper and cook until chicken registers 165°F.
6. Remove chicken and vegetables from the griddle and serve with warm tortillas.

NUTRITION: Calories: 408, Sodium: 664 mg, Dietary Fiber: 5.5 g, Fat: 18.3g, Carbs:37.1g, Protein: 25.9g.

Hawaiian Chicken Skewers

Preparation time: Time: 1 hour 10 minutes
Cooking Time: 15 minutes
Servings: 4 - 5

Ingredients:

- lb. boneless, skinless chicken breast, cut into 1 ½ inch cubes
- cups pineapple, cut into 1 ½ inch cubes
- large green peppers, cut into 1 ½ inch pieces
- 1 large red onion, cut into 1 ½ inch pieces
- 2 tablespoons olive oil, to coat veggies
- For the marinade:
- 1/3 cup tomato paste
- 1/3 cup brown sugar, packed
- 1/3 cup soy sauce
- 1/4 cup pineapple juice
- 2 tablespoons olive oil
- 1 1/2 tablespoon mirin or rice wine vinegar
- teaspoons garlic cloves, minced
- 1 tablespoon ginger, minced
- 1/2 teaspoon sesame oil
- Pinch of sea salt
- Pinch of ground black pepper
- 10 wooden skewers, for assembly

DIRECTIONS:

1. Combine marinade ingredients in a mixing bowl until smooth. Reserve a 1/2 cup of the marinade in the refrigerator.
2. Add chicken and remaining marinade to a sealable plastic bag and refrigerate for 1 hour.
3. Soak 10 wooden skewer sticks in water for 1 hour.
4. Preheat the griddle to medium heat.
5. Add red onion, bell pepper and pineapple to a mixing bowl with 2 tablespoons olive oil and toss to coat.
6. Thread red onion, bell pepper, pineapple and chicken onto the skewers until all of the chicken has been used.
7. Place skewers on griddle and grab your reserved marinade from the refrigerator; cook for 5 minutes then brush with remaining marinade and rotate.
8. Brush again with marinade and sear about 5 additional minutes or until chicken reads 165°F on a meat thermometer.
9. Serve warm.

NUTRITION: Calories: 311, Sodium: 1116 mg, Dietary Fiber: 4.2 g, Fat: 8.8 g, Carbs: 38.1 g, Protein: 22.8g.

Fiery Italian Chicken Skewers

Preparation time: 1 hour 20 minutes

Cooking Time: 20 minutes

Servings: 2 -4

INGREDIENTS:

- 10 boneless, skinless chicken thighs, cut into chunks
- large red onion, cut into wedges
- 1 large red pepper, stemmed, seeded, and cut into chunks
- For the marinade:
- 1/3 cup toasted pine nuts
- 1 1/2 cups sliced roasted red peppers
- hot cherry peppers, stemmed and seeded, or to taste
- 1 cup packed fresh basil leaves, plus more to serve
- cloves garlic, peeled
- 1/4 cup grated Parmesan cheese
- 1 tablespoon paprika
- extra virgin olive oil, as needed

DIRECTIONS:

1. Combine the toasted pine nuts, roasted red peppers, hot cherry peppers, basil, garlic, Parmesan, and paprika in a food processor or blender and process until well-combined.

2. Add in olive oil until the pesto reaches a thin consistency in order to coat the chicken as a marinade.

3. Transfer half of the pesto to a large sealable plastic bag, and reserve the other half for serving.

4. Add the chicken thigh chunks to the bag of pesto, seal, and massage the bag to coat the chicken.

5. Refrigerate for 1 hour.

6. Preheat griddle to medium-high heat and brush with olive oil.

7. Thread the chicken cubes, red onion, and red pepper onto metal skewers.

8. Brush the chicken with the reserved pesto.

9. Cook until the chicken reaches an internal temperature of 165°F; about 5 minutes per side. Serve warm with your favorite salad or vegetables!

NUTRITION: Calories: 945, Sodium: 798 mg, Dietary Fiber: 3.2 g, Fat: 46.7 g, Carbs: 14.7g, Protein: 112.2g.

Chicken Thighs with Ginger-Sesame Glaze

Preparation time: time: 10 minutes
Cooking Time: 20 minutes
Servings: 4 - 8

INGREDIENTS:

- 8 boneless, skinless chicken thighs
- For the glaze:
- 3 tablespoons dark brown sugar
- 2 1/2 tablespoons soy sauce
- tablespoon fresh garlic, minced
- teaspoons sesame seeds
- 1 teaspoon fresh ginger, minced
- 1 teaspoon sambal oelek
- 1/3 cup scallions, thinly sliced
- Non-stick cooking spray

DIRECTIONS:

1. Combine glaze ingredients in a large mixing bowl; separate and reserve half for serving.
2. Add chicken to bowl and toss to coat well.
3. Preheat the griddle to medium-high heat.
4. Coat with cooking spray.
5. Cook chicken for 6 minutes on each side or until done.
6. Transfer chicken to plates and drizzle with remaining glaze to serve.

NUTRITION: Calories: 301, Sodium: 413 mg, Dietary Fiber: 0.3 g, Fat: 11.2g, Carbs: 4.7g, Protein: 42.9g.

Honey Sriracha Griddle Chicken Thighs

Preparation time: 5 minutes
Cooking Time: 35 minutes
Servings: 6

INGREDIENTS:

- lbs. boneless chicken thighs
- 3 tablespoons butter, unsalted
- tablespoon fresh ginger, minced
- garlic cloves, minced
- 1/4 teaspoon smoked paprika
- 1/4 teaspoon chili powder
- tablespoons honey
- tablespoons Sriracha
- tablespoon lime juice

DIRECTIONS:

1. Preheat griddle to medium high.
2. Melt butter in a small saucepan on medium low heat; when melted add ginger and garlic. Stir until fragrant, about 2 minutes.
3. Fold in smoked paprika, ground cloves, honey, Sriracha and lime juice. Stir to combine, turn heat to medium and simmer for 5 minutes.
4. Rinse and pat chicken thighs dry.
5. Season with salt and pepper on both sides.
6. Spray griddle with non-stick cooking spray.
7. Place chicken thighs on griddle, skin side down first. Griddle for 5 minutes. Flip the chicken over and griddle on the other side for 5 minutes.
8. Continue to cook chicken, flipping every 3 minutes, so it doesn't burn, until the internal temperature reads 165ºF on a meat thermometer.
9. During the last 5 minutes of griddling brush the glaze on both sides of the chicken.
10. Remove from griddle and serve warm.

NUTRITION: Calories: 375, Sodium: 221 mg, Dietary Fiber: 0.3g, Fat: 22.5g, Carbs: 14.7g Protein: 32g

Buffalo Chicken Wings

Preparation time: time: 10 minutes

Cooking Time: 20 minutes

Servings: 6 - 8

INGREDIENTS:

- tablespoon sea salt
- teaspoon ground black pepper
- teaspoon garlic powder
- lbs. chicken wings
- tablespoons unsalted butter
- 1/3 cup buffalo sauce, like Moore's
- 1 tablespoon apple cider vinegar
- 1 tablespoon honey

DIRECTIONS:

1. Combine salt, pepper and garlic powder in a large mixing bowl.
2. Toss the wings with the seasoning mixture to coat.
3. Preheat griddle to medium heat.
4. Place the wings on the griddle; make sure they are touching so the meat stays moist on the bone while griddling.
5. Flip wings every 5 minutes, for a total of 20 minutes of cooking.
6. Heat the butter, buffalo sauce, vinegar and honey in a saucepan over low heat; whisk to combine well.
7. Add wings to a large mixing bowl, toss the wings with the sauce to coat.
8. Turn griddle up to medium high and place wings back on the griddle until the skins crisp; about 1 to 2 minutes per side.
9. Add wings back into the bowl with the sauce and toss to serve.

NUTRITION: Calories: 410, Sodium: 950 mg, Dietary Fiber: 0.2 g, Fat: 21.3g, Carbs: 2.7g, Protein: 49.4g.

Chicken Wings with Sweet Red Chili and Peach Glaze

Preparation time: time: 15 minutes
Cooking Time: 30 minutes
Servings: 4

INGREDIENTS:

- (12 oz.) jar peach preserves
- cup sweet red chili sauce
- 1 teaspoon lime juice
- 1 tablespoon fresh cilantro, minced
- 1 (2-1/2 lb.) bag chicken wing sections
- Non-stick cooking spray

DIRECTIONS:

1. Mix preserves, red chili sauce, lime juice and cilantro in mixing bowl. Divide in half, and place one half aside for serving.
2. Preheat griddle to medium heat and spray with non-stick cooking spray.
3. Cook wings for 25 minutes turning several times until juices run clear.
4. Remove wings from griddle, toss in a bowl to coat wings with remaining glaze.
5. Return wings to griddle and cook for an additional 3 to 5 minutes turning once.
6. Serve warm with your favorite dips and side dishes!

NUTRITION: Calories: 790, Sodium: 643 mg, Dietary Fiber: 1 g, Fat: 16.9 g, Carbs: 87.5g, Protein: 66g.

Yellow Curry Chicken Wings

Preparation time: time: 35 minutes
Cooking Time: 30 minutes to 1 hour
Servings: 6

INGREDIENTS:

- 2 lbs. chicken wings
- For the marinade:
- 1/2 cup Greek yogurt, plain
- tablespoon mild yellow curry powder
- tablespoon olive oil
- ½ teaspoon sea salt
- ½ teaspoon black pepper
- 1 teaspoon red chili flakes

DIRECTIONS:

1. Rinse and pat wings dry with paper towels.
2. Whisk marinade ingredients together in a large mixing bowl until well-combined.
3. Add wings to bowl and toss to coat.
4. Cover bowl with plastic wrap and chill in the refrigerator for 30 minutes.
5. Preparation time are one side of the griddle for medium heat and the other side on medium-high.
6. Working in batches, griddle wings over medium heat, turning occasionally, until skin starts to brown; about 12 minutes.
7. Move wings to medium-high area of griddle for 5 minutes on each side to char until cooked through; meat thermometer should register 165°F when touching the bone.
8. Transfer wings to a platter and serve warm.

NUTRITION: Calories: 324, Sodium: 292 mg, Dietary Fiber: 0.4 g, Fat: 14g, Carbs: 1.4g, Protein: 45.6g.

Korean Griddle Chicken Wings with Scallion

Preparation time: time: 30 minutes
Cooking Time: 30 minutes to 1 hour
Servings: 6

INGREDIENTS:

- 2 pounds chicken wings (flats and drumettes attached or separated)
- For the marinade:
- tablespoon olive oil
- teaspoon sea salt, plus more
- 1/2 teaspoon black pepper
- 1/2 cup gochujang, Korean hot pepper paste
- 1 scallion, thinly sliced, for garnish

DIRECTIONS:

1. Rinse and pat wings dry with paper towels.
2. Whisk marinade ingredients together in a large mixing bowl until well-combined.
3. Add wings to bowl and toss to coat.
4. Cover bowl with plastic wrap and chill in the refrigerator for 30 minutes.
5. Preparation time are one side of the griddle for medium heat and the other side on medium-high.
6. Working in batches, cook wings over medium heat, turning occasionally, until skin starts to brown; about 12 minutes.
7. Move wings to medium-high area of griddle for 5 minutes on each side to sear until cooked through; meat thermometer should register 165°F when touching the bone.
8. Transfer wings to a platter, garnish with scallions, and serve warm with your favorite dipping sauces.

NUTRITION: Calories: 312, Sodium: 476 mg, Dietary Fiber: 0.4 g, Fat: 13.5g, Carbs: 1.1g, Protein: 43.9g.

Kale Caesar Salad with Seared Chicken

Preparation time: time: 10 minutes
Cooking Time: 8 minutes
Servings: 1

INGREDIENTS:

- chicken breast
- 1 teaspoon garlic powder
- ½ teaspoon black pepper
- ½ teaspoon sea salt
- kale leaves, chopped
- shaved parmesan, for serving
- For the dressing:
- 1 tablespoon mayonnaise
- 1/2 tablespoon Dijon mustard
- ½ teaspoon garlic powder
- 1/2 teaspoon Worcestershire sauce
- 1/4 lemon, juice of (or 1/2 a small lime)
- ¼ teaspoon anchovy paste
- Pinch of sea salt
- Pinch of black pepper

DIRECTIONS:

1. Mix garlic powder, black pepper, and sea salt in a small mixing bowl. Coat chicken with seasoning mix.
2. Preheat griddle to medium-high heat.
3. Sear chicken on each side for 7 minutes or until a meat thermometer reads 165°F when inserted in the thickest part of the breast.
4. Whisk all of the dressing ingredients together.
5. Plate your kale and pour the dressing over, and toss to combine.
6. Cut the chicken on a diagonal and place on top of the salad. Garnish with shaved parmesan, and serve.

NUTRITION: Calories: 643, Sodium:1549 mg, Dietary Fiber: 3.8 g, Fat: 18.6g, Carbs: 26.3g, Protein: 93.3g.

Seared Chicken with Fruit Salsa

Preparation time: time: 1 hour
Cooking Time: 20 minutes
Servings: 4

INGREDIENTS:

- boneless, skinless chicken breasts
- For the marinade:
- 1/2 cup fresh lemon juice
- 1/2 cup soy sauce
- tablespoon fresh ginger, minced
- 1 tablespoon lemon pepper seasoning
- garlic cloves, minced
- For the salsa:
- 1 1/2 cups pineapple, chopped
- 3/4 cup kiwi fruit, chopped
- 1/2 cup mango, chopped
- 1/2 cup red onion, finely chopped
- tablespoons fresh cilantro, chopped
- 1 small jalapeño pepper, seeded and chopped
- 1 1/2 teaspoons ground cumin
- 1/4 teaspoon sea salt
- 1/8 teaspoon black pepper
- ½ teaspoon olive oil, more for brushing griddle

DIRECTIONS:

1. Combine marinade ingredients in a large sealable plastic bag.
2. Add chicken to bag, seal, and toss to coat. Marinate in refrigerator for 1 hour.
3. Combine salsa ingredients in a mixing bowl and toss gently to combine. Set aside until ready to serve.
4. Preheat the griddle to medium heat.
5. Remove chicken from bag and discard marinade.
6. Brush griddle with olive oil and cook chicken for 7 minutes on each side or until chicken is cooked through.
7. Serve chicken topped with salsa alongside your favorite side dishes.

NUTRITION: Calories: 391, Sodium: 2051 mg, Dietary Fiber: 3.7 g, Fat: 12.3g, Carbs:23.6g, Protein: 46.1g.

Teriyaki Chicken and Veggie Rice Bowls

Preparation time: time: 8 hours 10 minutes

Cooking Time: 20 minutes

Servings: 4

INGREDIENTS:

- bag brown rice
- For the skewers:
- boneless skinless chicken breasts, cubed
- 1 red onion, quartered
- 1 red pepper, cut into cube slices
- 1 green pepper, cut into cube slices
- 1/2 pineapple, cut into cubes
- For the marinade:
- 1/4 cup light soy sauce
- 1/4 cup sesame oil
- 1 tablespoon ginger, fresh grated
- 1 garlic clove, crushed
- 1/2 lime, juiced

DIRECTIONS:

1. Whisk the marinade ingredients together in a small mixing bowl.
2. Add chicken and marinade to a resealable plastic bag, seal and toss well to coat.
3. Refrigerate for one hour or overnight.
4. Preheat the griddle to medium-high heat.
5. Thread the chicken and the cubed veggies onto 8 metal skewers and cook for 8 minutes on each side until seared and cooked through.
6. Portion rice out into bowls and top with two skewers each, and enjoy!

NUTRITION: Calories: 477, Sodium: 362 mg, Dietary Fiber: 3.8 g, Fat: 20.6g, Carbs:48.1g, Protein: 26.1g.

Chicken Satay with Almond Butter Sauce

Preparation time: 2 hours 20 minutes
Cooking Time: 8 minutes
Servings: 4

INGREDIENTS:

- lb. boneless, skinless chicken thighs, cut into thin strips
- Olive oil, for brushing
- For the marinade:
- 1/2 cup canned light coconut milk
- 1/2 lime, juiced
- 1 tablespoon honey
- teaspoons soy sauce
- 1 1/2 teaspoons fish sauce
- 1/2 teaspoon red chili flakes
- teaspoons ginger, grated
- 1 clove of garlic, grated
- 1/2 teaspoon curry powder
- 1/4 teaspoon ground coriander
- For the almond butter sauce:
- 1/4 cup almond butter
- 1/4 cup water
- 2 tablespoons canned, light coconut milk
- 1 tablespoon honey
- 1/2 lime, juiced
- 1 teaspoon fish sauce
- 1 teaspoon fresh grated ginger
- 1/2 teaspoon low sodium soy sauce
- 1/2 teaspoon Sriracha

DIRECTIONS:

1. Whisk together all of the ingredients for the marinade in a medium mixing bowl.
2. Add chicken to mixing bowl and toss to coat.
3. Cover and refrigerate 2 hours or overnight.
4. Preheat griddle to medium high heat and brush with olive oil.
5. Thread the chicken strips onto metal skewers.
6. Place the chicken skewers on the **Prepa**red griddle and cook 3 minutes, rotate, and cook another 4 minutes or until the chicken is cooked through.
7. Whisk together all of the ingredients for the almond butter sauce in a small saucepan.
8. Bring the sauce to a boil on medium heat, then lower to medium low and simmer for 1 to 2 minutes or until the sauce thickens.
9. Serve chicken satay warm with the almond butter sauce and enjoy.

NUTRITION: Calories: 347, Sodium: 743 mg, Dietary Fiber: 1.2g, Fat: 19.7g, Carbs: 8.6g, Protein: 34.3g.

Chicken Fried Rice

Preparation time: time: 10 minutes
Cooking Time: 20 minutes
Servings: 4

INGREDIENTS:

- 2 boneless, skinless chicken breasts, cut into small pieces
- cups long grain rice, cooked and allowed to air dry
- 1/3 cup soy sauce
- yellow onion, finely chopped
- cloves garlic, finely chopped
- cups petite peas
- carrots sliced into thin rounds
- 1/2 cup corn kernels
- 1/4 cup vegetable oil
- tablespoons butter

DIRECTIONS:

1. Preheat griddle to medium-high.
2. Add the vegetable oil to the griddle.
3. When the oil is shimmering, add the onion, carrot, peas, and corn.
4. Cook for several minutes, until lightly charred.
5. Add the chicken and cook until just browned.
6. Add the rice, soy sauce, garlic, and butter.
7. Toss until the rice is tender and the vegetables are just softened.
8. Serve immediately.

NUTRITION: Calories: 485, Sodium: 1527 mg, Dietary Fiber: 4.7g, Fat: 20.8g, Carbs: 60.9g Protein: 13.4g

TURKEY RECIPES

Herb Roasted Turkey

Preparation Time: 15 Minutes
Cooking Time: 3 Hours 30 Minutes
Servings: 12

INGREDIENTS:

- 14 pounds turkey, cleaned
- 2 tablespoons chopped mixed herbs
- Pork and poultry rub as needed
- ¼ teaspoon ground black pepper
- 3 tablespoons butter, unsalted, melted
- 8 tablespoons butter, unsalted, softened
- 2 cups chicken broth

DIRECTIONS:

1. Clean the turkey by removing the giblets, wash it inside out, pat dry with paper towels, then place it on a roasting pan and tuck the turkey wings by tiring with butcher's string.
2. Switch on the griddle, set the temperature to 325 degrees F and let it preheat for a minimum of 15 minutes.
3. Meanwhile, **prepare** herb butter and for this, take a small bowl, place the softened butter in it, add black pepper and mixed herbs and beat until fluffy.
4. Place some of the **Prepare** herb butter underneath the skin of turkey by using a handle of a wooden spoon, and massage the skin to distribute butter evenly.
5. Then rub the exterior of the turkey with melted butter, season with pork and poultry rub, and pour the broth in the roasting pan.
6. When the griddle has preheated, open the lid, place roasting pan containing turkey on the griddle grate, shut the griddle and smoke for 3 hours and 30 minutes until the internal temperature reaches 165 degrees F and the top has turned golden brown.
7. When done, transfer turkey to a cutting board, let it rest for 30 minutes, then carve it into slices and serve.

NUTRITION: Calories: 154.6 Fat: 3.1 g Carbs: 8.4 g Protein: 28.8 g

Turkey Legs

Preparation Time: 10 Minutes
Cooking Time: 5 Hours
Servings: 4

INGREDIENTS:

- 4 turkey legs
- For the Brine:
- ½ cup curing salt
- 1 tablespoon whole black peppercorns
- 1 cup BBQ rub
- ½ cup brown sugar
- 2 bay leaves
- 2 teaspoons liquid smoke
- 16 cups of warm water
- 4 cups ice
- 8 cups of cold water

DIRECTIONS:

1. **Prepare** the brine and for this, take a large stockpot, place it over high heat, pour warm water in it, add peppercorn, bay leaves, and liquid smoke, stir in salt, sugar, and BBQ rub and bring it to a boil.
2. Remove pot from heat, bring it to room temperature, then pour in cold water, add ice cubes and let the brine chill in the refrigerator.
3. Then add turkey legs in it, submerge them completely, and let soak for 24 hours in the refrigerator.
4. After 24 hours, remove turkey legs from the brine, rinse well and pat dry with paper towels.
5. When ready to cook, switch on the griddle, set the temperature to 250 degrees F and let it preheat for a minimum of 15 minutes.
6. When the griddle has preheated, open the lid, place turkey legs on the griddle grate, shut the griddle, and smoke for 5 hours until nicely browned and the internal temperature reaches 165 degrees F. Serve immediately.

NUTRITION: Calories: 416 Fat: 13.3 g Carbs: 0 g Protein: 69.8 g

Turkey Breast

Preparation Time: 12 Hours
Cooking Time: 8 Hours
Servings: 6

INGREDIENTS:

- For the Brine:
- 2 pounds turkey breast, deboned
- 2 tablespoons ground black pepper
- ¼ cup salt
- 1 cup brown sugar
- 4 cups cold water
- For the BBQ Rub:
- 2 tablespoons dried onions
- 2 tablespoons garlic powder
- ¼ cup paprika
- 2 tablespoons ground black pepper
- 1 tablespoon salt
- 2 tablespoons brown sugar
- 2 tablespoons red chili powder
- 1 tablespoon cayenne pepper
- 2 tablespoons sugar
- 2 tablespoons ground cumin

DIRECTIONS:

1. **Prepare** the brine and for this, take a large bowl, add salt, black pepper, and sugar in it, pour in water, and stir until sugar has dissolved.
2. Place turkey breast in it, submerge it completely and let it soak for a minimum of 12 hours in the refrigerator.
3. Meanwhile, **Prepare** the BBQ rub and for this, take a small bowl, place all of its ingredients in it and then stir until combined, set aside until required.
4. Then remove turkey breast from the brine and season well with the **Prepare** BBQ rub.
5. When ready to cook, switch on the griddle, set the temperature to 180 degrees F and let it preheat for a minimum of 15 minutes.
6. When the griddle has preheated, open the lid, place turkey breast on the griddle grate, shut the griddle, change the smoking temperature to 225 degrees F, and smoke for 8 hours until the internal temperature reaches 160 degrees F.
7. When done, transfer turkey to a cutting board, let it rest for 10 minutes, then cut it into slices and serve.

NUTRITION: Calories: 250 Fat: 5 g Carbs: 31 g Protein: 18 g

Smoked Whole Turkey

Preparation Time: 10 minutes

Cooking Time: 5 hours

Servings: 6

INGREDIENTS:

- 1 (10- to 12-pound) turkey, giblets removed
- Extra-virgin olive oil, for rubbing
- ¼ cup poultry seasoning
- 8 tablespoons (1 stick) unsalted butter, melted
- ½ cup apple juice
- 2 teaspoons dried sage
- 2 teaspoons dried thyme

DIRECTIONS:

1. Supply your griddle follow the manufacturer's specific start-up procedure. Preheat, with the lid closed, to 250°F.

2. Rub the turkey with oil and season with the poultry seasoning inside and out, getting under the skin.

3. In a bowl, combine the melted butter, apple juice, sage, and thyme to use for basting.

4. Put the turkey in a roasting pan, place on the griddle, close the lid, and griddle for 5 to 6 hours, basting every hour, until the skin is brown and crispy, or until a meat thermometer inserted in the thickest part of the thigh reads 165°F.

5. Let the turkey meat rest for about 15 to 20 minutes before carving.

NUTRITION: Calories: 180 Carbs: 3g Fat: 2g Protein: 39g

Savory-Sweet Turkey Legs

Preparation Time: 10 minutes
Cooking Time: 5 hours
Servings: 4

INGREDIENTS:

- 1-gallon hot water
- 1 cup curing salt (such as Morton Tender Quick)
- ¼ cup packed light brown sugar
- 1 teaspoon freshly ground black pepper
- 1 teaspoon ground cloves
- 1 bay leaf
- 2 teaspoons liquid smoke
- 4 turkey legs
- Mandarin Glaze, for serving

DIRECTIONS:

1. In a huge container with a lid, stir together the water, curing salt, brown sugar, pepper, cloves, bay leaf, and liquid smoke until the salt and sugar are dissolved; let come to room temperature.
2. Submerge the turkey legs in the seasoned brine, cover, and refrigerate overnight.
3. When ready to smoke, remove the turkey legs from the brine and rinse them; discard the brine.
4. Supply your griddle Preheat, with the lid closed, to 225°F.
5. Arrange the turkey legs on the griddle, close the lid, and smoke for 4 to 5 hours, or until dark brown and a meat thermometer inserted in the thickest part of the meat reads 165°F.
6. Serve with Mandarin Glaze on the side or drizzled over the turkey legs.

NUTRITION: Calories: 190 Carbs: 1g Fat: 9g Protein: 24g

Marinated Smoked Turkey Breast

Preparation Time: 15 minutes

Cooking Time: 4 hours

Servings: 6

INGREDIENTS:

- 1 (5 pounds) boneless chicken breast
- 4 cups water
- 2 tablespoons kosher salt
- 1 teaspoon Italian seasoning
- 2 tablespoons honey
- 1 tablespoon cider vinegar
- Rub:
- ½ teaspoon onion powder
- 1 teaspoon paprika
- 1 teaspoon salt
- 1 teaspoon ground black pepper
- 1 tablespoon brown sugar
- ½ teaspoon garlic powder
- 1 teaspoon oregano

DIRECTIONS:

1. In a huge container, combine the water, honey, cider vinegar, Italian seasoning and salt.

2. Add the chicken breast and toss to combine. Cover the bowl and place it in the refrigerator and chill for 4 hours.

3. Rinse the chicken breast with water and pat dry with paper towels.

4. In another mixing bowl, combine the brown sugar, salt, paprika, onion powder, pepper, oregano and garlic.

5. Generously season the chicken breasts with the rub mix.

6. Preheat the griddle to 225°F with lid closed for 15 minutes.

7. Arrange the turkey breast into a griddle rack. Place the griddle rack on the griddle.

8. Smoke for about 3 to 4 hours or until the internal temperature of the turkey breast reaches 165°F.

9. Remove the chicken breast from heat and let them rest for a few minutes. Serve.

NUTRITION: Calories 903 Fat: 34g Carbs: 9.9g Protein 131.5g

Maple Bourbon Turkey

Preparation Time: 15 minutes
Cooking Time: 3 hours
Servings: 8

INGREDIENTS:

- 1 (12 pounds) turkey
- 8 cup chicken broth
- 1 stick butter (softened)
- 1 teaspoon thyme
- 2 garlic cloves (minced)
- 1 teaspoon dried basil
- 1 teaspoon pepper
- 1 teaspoon salt
- 1 tablespoon minced rosemary
- 1 teaspoon paprika
- 1 lemon (wedged)
- 1 onion
- 1 orange (wedged)
- 1 apple (wedged)
- Maple Bourbon Glaze:
- ¾ cup bourbon
- 1/2 cup maple syrup
- 1 stick butter (melted)
- 1 tablespoon lime

DIRECTIONS:

1. Wash the turkey meat inside and out under cold running water.
2. Insert the onion, lemon, orange and apple into the turkey cavity.
3. In a mixing bowl, combine the butter, paprika, thyme, garlic, basil, pepper, salt, basil and rosemary.
4. Brush the turkey generously with the herb butter mixture.
5. Set a rack into a roasting pan and place the turkey on the rack. Put a 5 cups of chicken broth into the bottom of the roasting pan.
6. Preheat the griddle to 350°F with lid closed for 15 minutes.
7. Place the roasting pan in the griddle and cook for 1 hour.
8. Meanwhile, combine all the maple bourbon glaze ingredients in a mixing bowl. Mix until well combined.
9. Baste the turkey with glaze mixture. Continue cooking, basting turkey every 30 minutes and adding more broth as needed for 2 hours, or until the internal temperature of the turkey reaches 165°F.
10. Take off the turkey from the griddle and let it rest for a few minutes. Cut into slices and serve.

NUTRITION: Calories 1536 Fat 58.6g Carbs: 24g Protein 20.1g

Thanksgiving Turkey

Preparation Time: 15 minutes

Cooking Time: 4 hours

Servings: 6

INGREDIENTS:

- 2 cups butter (softened)
- 1 tablespoon cracked black pepper
- 2 teaspoons kosher salt
- 2 tablespoons freshly chopped rosemary
- 2 tablespoons freshly chopped parsley
- 2 tablespoons freshly chopped sage
- 2 teaspoons dried thyme
- 6 garlic cloves (minced)
- 1 (18 pound) turkey

DIRECTIONS:

1. In a mixing bowl, combine the butter, sage, rosemary, 1 teaspoon black pepper, 1 teaspoon salt, thyme, parsley and garlic.
2. Use your fingers to loosen the skin from the turkey.
3. Generously, Rub butter mixture under the turkey skin and all over the turkey as well. 4. Season turkey generously with herb mix. 5. Preheat the griddle to 300°F with lid closed for 15 minutes.
4. Place the turkey on the griddle and roast for about 4 hours, or until the turkey thigh temperature reaches 160°F.
5. Take out the turkey meat from the griddle and let it rest for a few minutes. Cut into sizes and serve.

NUTRITION: Calories 278 Fat 30.8g Carbs: 1.6g Protein 0.6g

Spatchcock Smoked Turkey

Preparation Time: 15 minutes
Cooking Time: 4 hours 3 minutes
Servings: 6

INGREDIENTS:

- 1 (18 pounds) turkey
- 2 tablespoons finely chopped fresh parsley
- 1 tablespoon finely chopped fresh rosemary
- 2 tablespoons finely chopped fresh thyme
- ½ cup melted butter
- 1 teaspoon garlic powder
- 1 teaspoon onion powder
- 1 teaspoon ground black pepper
- 2 teaspoons salt or to taste
- 2 tablespoons finely chopped scallions

DIRECTIONS:

1. Remove the turkey giblets and rinse turkey, in and out, under cold running water.
2. Place the turkey on a working surface, breast side down. Use a poultry shear to cut the turkey along both sides of the backbone to remove the turkey back bone.
3. Flip the turkey over, back side down. Now, press the turkey down to flatten it.
4. In a mixing bowl, combine the parsley, rosemary, scallions, thyme, butter, pepper, salt, garlic and onion powder.
5. Rub butter mixture over all sides of the turkey.
6. Preheat your griddle to HIGH (450°F) with lid closed for 15 minutes.
7. Place the turkey directly on the griddle grate and cook for 30 minutes. Reduce the heat to 300°F and cook for an additional 4 hours, or until the internal temperature of the thickest part of the thigh reaches 165°F.
8. Take out the turkey meat from the griddle and let it rest for a few minutes. Cut into sizes and serve.

NUTRITION: Calories: 780 Fat: 19g Carbs: 29.7g Protein 116.4g

Hoisin Turkey Wings

Preparation Time: 15 minutes

Cooking Time: 1 hour

Servings: 8

INGREDIENTS:

- 2 pounds turkey wings
- ½ cup hoisin sauce
- 1 tablespoon honey
- 2 teaspoons soy sauce
- 2 garlic cloves (minced)
- 1 teaspoon freshly grated ginger
- 2 teaspoons sesame oil
- 1 teaspoons pepper or to taste
- 1 teaspoons salt or to taste
- ¼ cup pineapple juice
- 1 tablespoon chopped green onions
- 1 tablespoon sesame seeds
- 1 lemon (cut into wedges)

DIRECTIONS:

1. In a huge container, combine the honey, garlic, ginger, soy, hoisin sauce, sesame oil, pepper and salt. Put all the mixture into a zip lock bag and add the wings. Refrigerate for 2 hours.

2. Remove turkey from the marinade and reserve the marinade. Let the turkey rest for a few minutes, until it is at room temperature.

3. Preheat your griddle to 300°F with the lid closed for 15 minutes.

4. Arrange the wings into a griddling basket and place the basket on the griddle.

5. Griddle for 1 hour or until the internal temperature of the wings reaches 165°F.

6. Meanwhile, pour the reserved marinade into a saucepan over medium-high heat. Stir in the pineapple juice.

7. Wait to boil then reduce heat and simmer for until the sauce thickens.

8. Brush the wings with sauce and cook for 6 minutes more. Remove the wings from heat.

9. Serve and garnish it with green onions, sesame seeds and lemon wedges.

NUTRITION: Calories: 115 Fat: 4.8g Carbs: 11.9g Protein 6.8g

Turkey Jerky

Preparation Time: 15 minutes

Cooking Time: 4 hours

Servings: 6

INGREDIENTS:

- Marinade:
- 1 cup pineapple juice
- ½ cup brown sugar
- 2 tablespoons sriracha
- 2 teaspoons onion powder
- 2 tablespoons minced garlic
- 2 tablespoons rice wine vinegar
- 2 tablespoons hoisin
- 1 tablespoon red pepper flakes
- 1 tablespoon coarsely ground black pepper flakes
- 2 cups coconut amino
- 2 jalapenos (thinly sliced)
- Meat:
- 3 pounds turkey boneless skinless breasts (sliced to ¼ inch thick)

DIRECTIONS:

1.   Pour the marinade mixture ingredients in a container and mix until the ingredients are well combined.

2.   Put the turkey slices in a gallon sized zip lock bag and pour the marinade into the bag. Massage the marinade into the turkey. Seal the bag and refrigerate for 8 hours.

3.   Remove the turkey slices from the marinade.

4.   Activate the griddle for smoking for 5 minutes until fire starts.

5.   Close the lid and preheat your griddle to 180°F,

6.   Remove the turkey slices from the marinade and pat them dry with a paper towel.

7.   Arrange the turkey slices on the griddle in a single layer. Smoke the turkey for about 3 to 4 hours, turning often after the first 2 hours of smoking. The jerky should be dark and dry when it is done.

8.   Remove the jerky from the griddle and let it sit for about 1 hour to cool. Serve immediately or store in refrigerator.

NUTRITION: Calories: 109 Carbs: 12g Fat: 1g Protein: 14g

Smoked Whole Turkey

Preparation Time: 20 Minutes

Cooking Time: 8 Hours

Servings: 6

INGREDIENTS:

- 1 Whole Turkey of about 12 to 16 lb.
- 1 Cup of your Favorite Rub
- 1 Cup of Sugar
- 1 Tablespoon of minced garlic
- ½ Cup of Worcestershire sauce
- 2 Tablespoons of Canola Oil

DIRECTIONS:

1. Thaw the Turkey and remove the giblets
2. Pour in 3 gallons of water in a non-metal bucket of about 5 gallons
3. Add the BBQ rub and mix very well
4. Add the garlic, the sugar and the Worcestershire sauce; then submerge the turkey into the bucket.
5. Refrigerate the turkey in the bucket for an overnight.
6. Place the Griddle on a High Smoke and smoke the Turkey for about 3 hours
7. Switch the griddling temp to about 350 degrees F; then push a metal meat thermometer into the thickest part of the turkey breast
8. Cook for about 4 hours; then take off the griddle and let rest for about 15 minutes
9. Slice the turkey, then serve and enjoy your dish!

NUTRITION: Calories: 165 Fat: 14g Carbs: 0.5g Protein: 15.2g

Smoked Turkey Breast

Preparation Time: 10 Minutes
Cooking Time: 1 Hour 30 minutes
Servings: 6

INGREDIENTS:

- For the Brine
- 1 Cup of kosher salt
- 1 Cup of maple syrup
- ¼ Cup of brown sugar
- ¼ Cup of whole black peppercorns
- 4 Cups of cold bourbon
- 1 and ½ gallons of cold water
- 1 Turkey breast of about 7 pounds
- For the Turkey
- 3 Tablespoons of brown sugar
- 1 and ½ tablespoons of smoked paprika
- 1 ½ teaspoons of chipotle chili powder
- 1 ½ teaspoons of garlic powder
- 1 ½ teaspoons of salt
- 1 and ½ teaspoons of black pepper
- 1 Teaspoon of onion powder
- ½ teaspoon of ground cumin
- 6 Tablespoons of melted unsalted butter

DIRECTIONS:

1. Before beginning; make sure that the bourbon; the water and the chicken stock are all cold
2. Now to make the brine, combine altogether the salt, the syrup, the sugar, the peppercorns, the bourbon, and the water in a large bucket.
3. Remove any pieces that are left on the turkey, like the neck or the giblets
4. Refrigerate the turkey meat in the brine for about 8 to 12 hours in a reseal able bag
5. Remove the turkey breast from the brine and pat dry with clean paper towels; then place it over a baking sheet and refrigerate for about 1 hour
6. Preheat your griddle to about 300°F;
7. In a bowl, mix the paprika with the sugar, the chili powder, the garlic powder, the salt, the pepper, the onion powder and the cumin, mixing very well to combine.
8. Carefully lift the skin of the turkey; then rub the melted butter over the meat
9. Rub the spice over the meat very well and over the skin
i. Smoke the turkey breast for about 1 ½ hours at a temperature of about 375°

NUTRITION: Calories: 94 Fat: 2g Carbs: 1g Protein: 18g

Whole Turkey

Preparation Time: 10 Minutes
Cooking Time: 7 Hours And 30 Minutes
Servings: 10

INGREDIENTS:

- 1 frozen whole turkey, giblets removed, thawed
- 2 tablespoons orange zest
- 2 tablespoons chopped fresh parsley
- 1 teaspoon salt
- 2 tablespoons chopped fresh rosemary
- 1 teaspoon ground black pepper
- 2 tablespoons chopped fresh sage
- 1 cup butter, unsalted, softened, divided
- 2 tablespoons chopped fresh thyme
- ½ cup water
- 14.5-ounce chicken broth

DIRECTIONS:

1. Open hopper of the griddle, add dry pallets, make sure ash-can is in place, then open the ash damper, power on the griddle and close the ash damper.
2. Set the temperature of the griddle to 180 degrees F, let preheat for 30 minutes or until the green light on the dial blinks that indicate griddle has reached to set temperature.
3. Meanwhile, **Prepare** the turkey and for this, tuck its wings under it by using kitchen twine.
4. Place ½ cup butter in a bowl, add thyme, parsley, and sage, orange zest, and rosemary, stir well until combined and then brush this mixture generously on the inside and outside of the turkey and season the external of turkey with salt and black pepper.
5. Place turkey on a roasting pan, breast side up, pour in broth and water, add the remaining butter in the pan, then place the pan on the griddle and shut with lid.
6. Smoke the turkey for 3 hours, then increase the temperature to 350 degrees F and continue smoking the turkey for 4 hours or until thoroughly cooked and the internal temperature of the turkey reaches to 165 degrees F, basting turkey with the dripping every 30 minutes, but not in the last hour.
7. When you are done, take off the roasting pan from the griddle and let the turkey rest for 20 minutes.
8. Carve turkey into pieces and serve.

NUTRITION: Calories: 146 Fat: 8 g Protein: 18 g Carbs: 1 g
Turkey Recipes

Herbed Turkey Breast

Preparation Time: 8 Hours And 10 Minutes
Cooking Time: 3 Hours
Servings: 12

INGREDIENTS:

- 7 pounds turkey breast, bone-in, skin-on, fat trimmed
- 3/4 cup salt
- 1/3 cup brown sugar
- 4 quarts water, cold
- For Herbed Butter:
- 1 tablespoon chopped parsley
- ½ teaspoon ground black pepper
- 8 tablespoons butter, unsalted, softened
- 1 tablespoon chopped sage
- ½ tablespoon minced garlic
- 1 tablespoon chopped rosemary
- 1 teaspoon lemon zest
- 1 tablespoon chopped oregano
- 1 tablespoon lemon juice

DIRECTIONS:

1. **Prepare** the brine and for this, pour water in a large container, add salt and sugar and stir well until salt and sugar has completely dissolved.
2. Add turkey breast in the brine, cover with the lid and let soak in the refrigerator for a minimum of 8 hours.
3. Then remove turkey breast from the brine, rinse well and pat dry with paper towels.
4. Open hopper of the griddle, add dry pallets, make sure ash-can is in place, then open the ash damper, power on the griddle and close the ash damper.
5. Set the temperature of the griddle to 350 degrees F, let preheat for 30 minutes or until the green light on the dial blinks that indicate griddle has reached to set temperature.
6. Meanwhile, take a roasting pan, pour in 1 cup water, then place a wire rack in it and place turkey breast on it.
7. **Prepare** the herb butter and for this, place butter in a heatproof bowl, add remaining ingredients for the butter and stir until just mix.
8. Loosen the skin of the turkey from its breast by using your fingers, then insert 2 tablespoons of **Prepare** herb butter on each side of the skin of the breastbone and spread it evenly, pushing out all the air pockets.
9. Place the remaining herb butter in the bowl into the microwave wave and heat for 1 minute or more at high heat setting or until melted.
i. Then brush melted herb butter on the outside of the turkey breast and place roasting pan containing turkey on the griddle.
ii. **Shut the griddle with lid and smoke for 2 hours and 30 minutes or until the turkey breast is nicely golden brown and the internal temperature of turkey reach to 165 degrees F, flipping the turkey and basting with melted herb butter after 1 hour and 30 minutes smoking.**
iii. **When done, transfer the turkey breast to a cutting board, let it rest for 15 minutes, then carve it into pieces and serve.**

NUTRITION: Calories: 97 Fat: 4 g Protein: 13 g Carbs: 1 g

Jalapeno Injection Turkey

Preparation Time: 15 Minutes

Cooking Time: 4 Hours And 10 Minutes

Servings: 4

INGREDIENTS:

- 15 pounds whole turkey, giblet removed
- ½ of medium red onion, peeled and minced
- 8 jalapeño peppers
- 2 tablespoons minced garlic
- 4 tablespoons garlic powder
- 6 tablespoons Italian seasoning
- 1 cup butter, softened, unsalted
- ¼ cup olive oil
- 1 cup chicken broth

DIRECTIONS:

1. Open hopper of the griddle, add dry pallets, make sure ash-can is in place, then open the ash damper, power on the griddle and close the ash damper.

2. Make the temperature of the griddle up to 200 degrees F, let preheat for 30 minutes or until the green light on the dial blinks that indicate griddle has reached to set temperature.

3. Meanwhile, place a large saucepan over medium-high heat, add oil and butter and when the butter melts, add onion, garlic, and peppers and cook for 3 to 5 minutes or until nicely golden brown.

4. Pour in broth, stir well, let the mixture boil for 5 minutes, then remove pan from the heat and strain the mixture to get just liquid.

5. Inject turkey generously with **Prepare** liquid, then spray the outside of turkey with butter spray and season well with garlic and Italian seasoning.

6. Place turkey on the griddle, shut with lid, and smoke for 30 minutes, then increase the temperature to 325 degrees F and continue smoking the turkey for 3 hours or until the internal temperature of turkey reach to 165 degrees F.

7. When done, transfer turkey to a cutting board, let rest for 5 minutes, then carve into slices and serve.

NUTRITION: Calories: 131 Fat: 7 g Protein: 13 g Carbs: 3 g

Smoked Turkey Mayo with Green Apple

Preparation Time: 20 minutes

Cooking Time: 4 hours 10 minutes

Servings: 10

INGREDIENTS:

- Whole turkey (4-lbs., 1.8-kg.)
- The Rub
- Mayonnaise – ½ cup
- Salt – ¾ teaspoon
- Brown sugar – ¼ cup
- Ground mustard – 2 tablespoons
- Black pepper – 1 teaspoon
- Onion powder – 1 ½ tablespoons
- Ground cumin – 1 ½ tablespoons
- Chili powder – 2 tablespoons
- Cayenne pepper – ½ tablespoon
- Old Bay Seasoning – ½ teaspoon
- The Filling
- Sliced green apples – 3 cups

DIRECTIONS:

1. Place salt, brown sugar, brown mustard, black pepper, onion powder, ground cumin, chili powder, cayenne pepper, and old bay seasoning in a bowl then mix well. Set aside.
2. Next, fill the turkey cavity with sliced green apples then baste mayonnaise over the turkey skin.
3. Sprinkle the dry spice mixture over the turkey then wrap with aluminum foil.
4. Marinate the turkey for at least 4 hours or overnight and store in the fridge to keep it fresh.
5. On the next day, remove the turkey from the fridge and thaw at room temperature.
6. Set the griddle for indirect heat then adjust the temperature to 275°F (135°C).
7. Unwrap the turkey and place in the griddle.
8. Smoke the turkey for 4 hours or until the internal temperature has reached 170°F (77°C).
9. Remove the smoked turkey from the griddle and serve.

NUTRITION: Calories: 340 Carbs: 40g Fat: 10g Protein: 21g

Buttery Smoked Turkey Beer

Preparation Time: 15 minutes

Cooking Time: 4 hours

Servings: 6

INGREDIENTS:

- Whole turkey (4-lbs., 1.8-kg.)
- The Brine
- Beer – 2 cans
- Salt – 1 tablespoon
- White sugar – 2 tablespoons
- Soy sauce – ¼ cup
- Cold water – 1 quart
- The Rub
- Unsalted butter – 3 tablespoons
- Smoked paprika – 1 teaspoon
- Garlic powder – 1 ½ teaspoons
- Pepper – 1 teaspoon
- Cayenne pepper – ¼ teaspoon

DIRECTIONS:

1. Pour beer into a container then add salt, white sugar, and soy sauce then stir well.

2. Put the turkey into the brine mixture cold water over the turkey. Make sure that the turkey is completely soaked.

3. Soak the turkey in the brine for at least 6 hours or overnight and store in the fridge to keep it fresh.

4. On the next day, remove the turkey from the fridge and take it out of the brine mixture.

5. Wash and rinse the turkey then pat it dry.

6. Set the griddle for indirect heat then adjust the temperature to 275°F (135°C).

7. Open the beer can then push it in the turkey cavity.

8. Place the seasoned turkey in the griddle and make a tripod using the beer can and the two turkey-legs.

9. Smoke the turkey for 4 hours or until the internal temperature has reached 170°F (77°C).

10. Once it is done, remove the smoked turkey from the griddle and transfer it to a serving dish.

NUTRITION: Calories: 229 Carbs: 34g Fat: 8g Protein: 3g

Barbecue Chili Smoked Turkey Breast

Preparation Time: 15 minutes
Cooking Time: 4 hours 20 minutes
Servings: 8

INGREDIENTS:

- Turkey breast (3-lb., 1.4-kg.)
- The Rub
- Salt – ¾ teaspoon
- Pepper – ½ teaspoon
- The Glaze
- Olive oil – 1 tablespoon
- Ketchup – ¾ cup
- White vinegar – 3 tablespoons
- Brown sugar – 3 tablespoons
- Smoked paprika – 1 tablespoon
- Chili powder – ¾ teaspoon
- Cayenne powder – ¼ teaspoon

DIRECTIONS:

1. Score the turkey breast at several places then sprinkle salt and pepper over it.
2. Let the seasoned turkey breast rest for approximately 10 minutes.
3. Set the griddle for indirect heat then adjust the temperature to 275°F (135°C).
4. Place the seasoned turkey breast in the griddle and smoke for 2 hours.
5. In the meantime, combine olive oil, ketchup, white vinegar, brown sugar, smoked paprika; chili powder, garlic powder, and cayenne pepper in a saucepan then stir until incorporated. Wait to simmer then remove from heat.
6. After 2 hours of smoking, baste the sauce over the turkey breast and continue smoking for another 2 hours.
7. Once the internal temperature of the smoked turkey breast has reached 170°F (77°C) remove from the griddle and wrap with aluminum foil.
8. Let the smoked turkey breast rest for approximately 15 minutes to 30 minutes then unwrap it.
9. Cut the smoked turkey breast into thick slices then serve.

NUTRITION: Calories: 290 Carbs: 2g Fat: 3g Protein: 63g

Hot Sauce Smoked Turkey Tabasco

Preparation Time: 20 minutes

Cooking Time: 4 hours 15 minutes

Servings: 8

INGREDIENTS:

- Whole turkey (4-lbs., 1.8-kg.)
- The Rub
- Brown sugar – ¼ cup
- Smoked paprika – 2 teaspoons
- Salt – 1 teaspoon
- Onion powder – 1 ½ teaspoons
- Oregano – 2 teaspoons
- Garlic powder – 2 teaspoons
- Dried thyme – ½ teaspoon
- White pepper – ½ teaspoon
- Cayenne pepper – ½ teaspoon
- The Glaze
- Ketchup – ½ cup
- Hot sauce – ½ cup
- Cider vinegar – 1 tablespoon
- Tabasco – 2 teaspoons
- Cajun spices – ½ teaspoon
- Unsalted butter – 3 tablespoons

DIRECTIONS:

1. Rub the turkey with 2 tablespoons of brown sugar, smoked paprika, salt, onion powder, garlic powder, dried thyme, white pepper, and cayenne pepper. Let the turkey rest for an hour.
2. Set the griddle for indirect heat then adjust the temperature to 275°F (135°C).
3. Place the seasoned turkey in the griddle and smoke for 4 hours.
4. In the meantime, place ketchup, hot sauce, cider vinegar, Tabasco, and Cajun spices in a saucepan then bring to a simmer.
5. Remove the sauce from heat and quickly add unsalted butter to the saucepan. Stir until melted.
6. After 4 hours of smoking, baste the Tabasco sauce over the turkey then continue smoking for 15 minutes.
7. Once the internal temperature of the smoked turkey has reached 170°F (77°C), remove from the griddle and place it on a serving dish.

NUTRITION: Calories: 160 Carbs: 2g Fat: 14g Protein: 7g

Cured Turkey Drumstick

Preparation Time: 20 minutes
Cooking Time: 2.5 hours to 3 hours
Servings: 3

INGREDIENTS:

- 3 fresh or thawed frozen turkey drumsticks
- 3 tablespoons extra virgin olive oil
- Brine component
- 4 cups of filtered water
- ¼Cup kosher salt
- ¼ cup brown sugar
- 1 teaspoon garlic powder
- Poultry seasoning 1 teaspoon
- 1/2 teaspoon red pepper flakes
- 1 teaspoon pink hardened salt

DIRECTIONS:

1. Put the salt water ingredients in a 1-gallon sealable bag. Add the turkey drumstick to the salt water and refrigerate for 12 hours.
2. After 12 hours, remove the drumstick from the saline, rinse with cold water, and pat dry with a paper towel.
3. Air dry the drumstick in the refrigerator without a cover for 2 hours.
4. Remove the drumsticks from the refrigerator and rub a tablespoon of extra virgin olive oil under and over each drumstick.
5. Set the griddle for indirect cooking and preheat to 250 degrees
6. Place the drumstick on the griddle and smoke at 250 ° F for 2 hours.
7. After 2 hours, increase griddle temperature to 325 ° F.
8. Cook the turkey drumstick at 325 ° F until the internal temperature of the thickest part of each drumstick is 180 ° F with an instant reading digital thermometer.
9. Place a smoked turkey drumstick under a loose foil tent for 15 minutes before eating.

NUTRITION: Calories: 278 Carbs: 0g Fat: 13g Protein: 37g

Tailgate Smoked Young Turkey

Preparation Time: 20 Minutes

Cooking Time: 4 To 4 Hours 30 Minutes

Servings: 6

INGREDIENTS:

- 1 fresh or thawed frozen young turkey
- 6 glasses of extra virgin olive oil with roasted garlic flavor
- 6 original Yang dry lab or poultry seasonings

DIRECTIONS:

1. Remove excess fat and skin from turkey breasts and cavities.
2. Slowly separate the skin of the turkey to its breast and a quarter of the leg, leaving the skin intact.
3. Apply olive oil to the chest, under the skin and on the skin.
4. Gently rub or season to the chest cavity, under the skin and on the skin.
5. Set up tailgate griddle for indirect cooking and smoking. Preheat to 225 ° F.
6. Put the turkey meat on the griddle with the chest up.
7. Suck the turkey for 4-4 hours at 225 ° F until the thickest part of the turkey's chest reaches an internal temperature of 170 ° F and the juice is clear.
8. Before engraving, place the turkey under a loose foil tent for 20 minutes

NUTRITION: Calories: 240 Carbs: 27g Fat: 9g Protein: 15g

Roast Turkey Orange

Preparation Time: 30 Minutes
Cooking Time: 2 hours 30 minutes
Servings:

INGREDIENTS:

- 1 Frozen Long Island turkey
- 3 tablespoons west
- 1 large orange, cut into wedges
- Three celery stems chopped into large chunks
- Half a small red onion, a quarter
- Orange sauce:
- 2 orange cups
- 2 tablespoons soy sauce
- 2 tablespoons orange marmalade
- 2 tablespoons honey
- 3 teaspoons grated raw

DIRECTIONS:

1. Remove the jibble from the turkey's cavity and neck and retain or discard for another use. Wash the duck and pat some dry paper towel.

2. Remove excess fat from tail, neck and cavity. Use a sharp scalpel knife tip to pierce the turkey's skin entirely, so that it does not penetrate the duck's meat, to help dissolve the fat layer beneath the skin.

3. Add the seasoning inside the cavity with one cup of rub or seasoning.

4. Season the outside of the turkey with the remaining friction or seasoning.

5. Fill the cavity with orange wedges, celery and onion. Duck legs are tied with butcher twine to make filling easier. Place the turkey's breast up on a small rack of shallow roast bread.

6. To make the sauce, mix the ingredients in the saucepan over low heat and cook until the sauce is thick and syrupy. Set aside and let cool.

7. Set the griddle for indirect cooking and preheat to 350 ° F.

8. Roast the turkey at 350 ° F for 2 hours.

9. After 2 hours, brush the turkey freely with orange sauce.

10. Roast the orange glass turkey for another 30 minutes, making sure that the inside temperature of the thickest part of the leg reaches 165 ° F.

11. Place turkey under loose foil tent for 20 minutes before serving.

12. Discard the orange wedge, celery and onion. Serve with a quarter of turkey with poultry scissors.

NUTRITION: Calories: 216 Carbs: 2g Fat: 11g Protein: 34g

Salmon Fillets with Basil Butter & Broccolini

Basil infused broccoli is the perfect way to elevate seared salmon. Healthy and delicious, this recipe is also easy to make on those busy weeknights when you still want a decadent tasting dinner.

Servings: 2 | **Preparation time:** time: 10 minutes | **Cooking TIME:** 12 minutes

INGREDIENTS:

- 2 (6 ounce) salmon fillets, skin removed
- 2 tablespoons butter, unsalted
- 2 basil leaves, minced
- 1 garlic clove, minced
- 6 ounces broccolini
- 2 teaspoons olive oil
- Sea salt, to taste

DIRECTIONS:

1. Blend butter, basil, and garlic together until well-incorporated. Form into a ball and place in refrigerator until ready to serve.
2. Preheat griddle to medium-high heat.
3. Season both sides of the salmon fillets with salt and set aside.
4. Add broccolini, a pinch of salt, and olive oil to a bowl, toss to coat, and set aside.
5. Brush griddle with olive oil, and cook salmon, skin side down, for 12 minutes. Turn the salmon and cook for an additional 4 minutes. Remove from the griddle and allow to rest while the broccolini cooks.
6. Add the broccolini to the griddle, turning occasionally, until slightly charred, about 6 minutes.
7. Top each salmon fillet with a slice of basil butter and serve with a side of broccolini.

Nutrition: Calories: 398, Sodium: 303mg, Dietary Fiber: 2.2g, Fat: 26.7g, Carbs: 6.2g, Protein: 35.6g.

Spiced Snapper with Mango and Red Onion Salad

Spiced snapper meats cool, crisp mango salad for one delicious way to griddle up lunch. Serve this gorgeous seafood feast with sparkling water with lemon and warm baguettes for a delicious lunch in the sun.

Servings: 4 | **Preparation time:** time: 10 minutes | **Cooking TIME:** 20 minutes

INGREDIENTS:

- 2 red snappers, cleaned
- Sea salt
- 1/3 cup tandoori spice
- Olive oil, plus more for griddle
- Extra-virgin olive oil, for drizzling
- Lime wedges, for serving
- For the salsa:
- 1 ripe but firm mango, peeled and chopped
- 1 small red onion, thinly sliced
- 1 bunch cilantro, coarsely chopped
- 3 tablespoons fresh lime juice

DIRECTIONS:

1. Toss mango, onion, cilantro, lime juice, and a big pinch of salt in a medium mixing bowl; drizzle with a bit of olive oil and toss again to coat.
2. Place snapper on a cutting board and pat dry with paper towels. Cut slashes crosswise on a diagonal along the body every 2" on both sides, with a sharp knife, cutting all the way down to the bones.
3. Season fish generously inside and out with salt. Coat fish with tandoori spice.
4. Preheat griddle medium-high heat and brush with oil.
5. Griddle fish for 10 minutes, undisturbed, until skin is puffed and charred.
6. Flip and griddle fish until the other side is lightly charred and skin is puffed, about 8 to 12 minutes.
7. Transfer to a platter.
8. Top with mango salad and serve with lime wedges.

NUTRITION: Calories: 211, Sodium: 170mg, Dietary Fiber: 2.5g, Fat: 5.4g, Carbs: 18.9g, Protein: 23.6g.

Honey-Lime Tilapia and Corn Foil Pack

The sweet taste of honey and citrus lime come together to infuse flaky tilapia with a flavor sensation out of this world. Serve these yummy foil packs with garden salads and your favorite sparkling beverage.

Servings: 4 | **Preparation time:** time: 10 minutes | **Cooking TIME:** 10 minutes

INGREDIENTS:

- 4 fillets tilapia
- 2 tablespoons honey
- 4 limes, thinly sliced
- 2 ears corn, shucked
- 2 tablespoons fresh cilantro leaves
- 1/4 cup olive oil
- Kosher salt
- Freshly ground black pepper

DIRECTIONS:

1. Preheat griddle to high.
2. Cut 4 squares of foil about 12" long.
3. Top each piece of foil with a piece of tilapia.
4. Brush tilapia with honey and top with lime, corn and cilantro.
5. Drizzle with olive oil and season with sea salt and pepper.
6. Cook until tilapia is cooked through and corn tender, about 15 minutes.

Nutrition: Calories: 319, Sodium: 92mg, Dietary Fiber: 4g, Fat: 14.7g, Carbs: 30.3g, Protein: 24g.

Halibut Fillets with Spinach and Olives

Fresh flaky fish is perfect served with salty olives and fresh spinach. This recipe makes for one quick and easy dinner any day of the week!

Servings: 4 | **Preparation time:** time: 10 minutes | **Cooking TIME:** 10 minutes

INGREDIENTS:

- 4 (6 ounce) halibut fillets
- 1/3 cup olive oil
- 4 cups baby spinach
- 1/4 cup lemon juice
- 2 ounces pitted black olives, halved
- 2 tablespoons flat leaf parsley, chopped
- 2 teaspoons fresh dill, chopped
- Lemon wedges, to serve

DIRECTIONS:

1. Preheat griddle to medium heat.
2. Toss spinach with lemon juice in a mixing bowl and set aside.
3. Brush fish with olive oil and cook for 3-4 minutes per side, or until cooked through.
4. Remove from heat, cover with foil and let rest for 5 minutes.
5. Add remaining oil and cook spinach for 2 minutes, or until just wilted. Remove from heat.
6. Toss with olives and herbs, then transfer to serving plates with fish, and serve with lemon wedges.

NUTRITION: Calories: 773, Sodium: 1112mg, Dietary Fiber: 1.4g, Fat: 36.6g, Carbs: 2.9g, Protein: 109.3g.

Gremolata Swordfish Skewers

Delicate, flaky swordfish makes for one delicious Griddle skewer! Serve your yummy swordfish with lemon chili pasta, salad, and Chardonnay or sparkling water with lemon.

Servings: 4 | **Preparation time:** time: 20 minutes | **Cooking TIME:** 10 minutes

INGREDIENTS:

- 1-1/2 lb. skinless swordfish fillet
- 2 teaspoons lemon zest
- 3 tablespoons lemon juice
- 1/2 cup finely chopped parsley
- 2 teaspoons garlic, minced
- 3/4 teaspoon sea salt
- 1/4 teaspoon black pepper
- 2 tablespoons extra-virgin olive oil, plus extra for serving
- 1/2 teaspoon red pepper flakes
- 3 lemons, cut into slices

DIRECTIONS:

1. Preheat griddle to medium-high.
2. Combine lemon zest, parsley, garlic, 1/4 teaspoon of the salt, and pepper in a small bowl with a fork to make gremolata and set aside.
3. Mix swordfish pieces with reserved lemon juice, olive oil, red pepper flakes, and remaining salt.
4. Thread swordfish and lemon slices, alternating each, onto the metal skewers.
5. Griddle skewers 8 to 10 minutes, flipping halfway through, or until fish is cooked through.
6. Place skewers on a serving platter and sprinkle with gremolata.
7. Drizzle with olive oil and serve.

NUTRITION: Calories: 333, Sodium: 554mg, Dietary Fiber: 0.5g, Fat: 16g, Carbs: 1.6g, Protein: 43.7g.

Lobster Tails with Lime Basil Butter

For one amazing dinner, fire up your outdoor griddle and you can griddle up lobster tails in less than 10 minutes. Serve them with Griddle vegetables, crab legs, and shrimp for a seafood feast.

Servings: 4 | **Preparation time:** time: 5 minutes | **Cooking TIME:** 6 minutes

INGREDIENTS:

- 4 lobster tails (cut in half lengthwise)
- 3 tablespoons olive oil
- Lime wedges (to serve)
- Sea salt, to taste
- For the lime basil butter:
- 1 stick unsalted butter, softened
- 1/2 bunch basil, roughly chopped
- 1 lime, zested and juiced
- 2 cloves garlic, minced
- 1/4 teaspoon red pepper flakes

DIRECTIONS:

1. Add the butter ingredients to a mixing bowl and combine; set aside until ready to use.
2. Preheat griddle to medium-high heat.
3. Drizzle the lobster tail halves with olive oil and season with salt and pepper.
4. Place the lobster tails, flesh-side down, on the griddle.
5. Allow to cook until opaque, about 3 minutes, flip and cook another 3 minutes.
6. Add a dollop of the lime basil butter during the last minute of cooking.
7. Serve immediately.

NUTRITION: Calories: 430, Sodium: 926mg, Dietary Fiber: 0.5g, Fat: 34.7g, Carbs: 2.4g, Protein: 28g.

Spiced Crab Legs

Crab legs with a twist! If you love spice, you'll love this recipe - but on the chance you just love crab legs you can also substitute chili for olive oil and try it hot and mild!

Servings: 4 | **Preparation time:** time: 5 minutes | **Cooking TIME:** 5 minutes

INGREDIENTS:

- 4 lbs. king crab legs, cooked
- 2 tablespoons chili oil

- **Directions:**
- Preheat griddle to high.
- Brush both sides of crab legs with chili oil and place on griddle. Tent with foil.
- Cook 4 to 5 minutes, turning once.
- Transfer to plates and serve with drawn butter.

NUTRITION: Calories: 518, Sodium: 4857mg, Dietary Fiber: 0g, Fat: 13.9g, Carbs: 0g, Protein: 87.1g.

Lump Crab Cakes

Cooking crab cakes on your outdoor griddle is a no brainer because of the perfectly controlled and even heat the flat top surface offers. These crab cakes are bursting with flavors the whole family will love.

Servings: 4 | **Preparation time:** time: 10 minutes | **Cooking TIME:** 15 minutes

INGREDIENTS:

- 1 lb. lump crab meat
- 1/2 cup panko breadcrumbs
- 1/3 cup mayonnaise
- 1 egg, beaten
- 2 tablespoons Dijon mustard
- 2 teaspoons Worcestershire sauce
- 1/2 teaspoon paprika
- 1/2 teaspoon salt
- 1/4 teaspoon black pepper
- 3 tablespoons vegetable oil

DIRECTIONS:

1. Preheat griddle to medium heat.
2. In a large bowl, combine the crab, breadcrumbs, mayo, egg, mustard Worcestershire sauce, paprika, salt and pepper. Mix well to combine.
3. Form the crab mixture into 4 large balls and flatten them slightly.
4. Add the oil to the griddle and cook the crab cakes for approximately 5 minutes per side or until browned and crispy. Serve immediately.

NUTRITION: Calories: 282, Sodium: 1205mg, Dietary Fiber: 0.6g, Fat: 27.4g, Carbs: 9.5g, Protein: 18.8g.

Spicy Griddle Jumbo Shrimp

Spicy Griddle shrimp is just out of this world! Top your favorite salads, yellow rice and vegetables, or even serve it on its own for griddling fun.

Servings: 6 | **Preparation time:** time: 15 minutes | **Cooking TIME:** 8 minutes

INGREDIENTS:

- 1-1/2 pounds uncooked jumbo shrimp, peeled and deveined
- For the marinade:
- 2 tablespoons fresh parsley
- 1 bay leaf, dried
- 1 teaspoon chili powder
- 1 teaspoon garlic powder
- 1/4 teaspoon cayenne pepper
- 1/4 cup olive oil
- 1/4 teaspoon salt
- 1/8 teaspoon pepper

DIRECTIONS:

1. Add marinade ingredients to a food processor and process until smooth.
2. Transfer marinade to a large mixing bowl.
3. Fold in shrimp and toss to coat; refrigerate, covered, 30 minutes.
4. Thread shrimp onto metal skewers.
5. Preheat griddle to medium heat.
6. Cook 5-6 minutes, flipping once, until shrimp turn opaque pink.
7. Serve immediately.

NUTRITION: Calories: 131, Sodium: 980mg, Dietary Fiber: 0.4g, Fat: 8.5g, Carbs: 1g, Protein: 13.7g.

Coconut Pineapple Shrimp Skewers

Creamy coconut and fresh pineapple come together to create a taste of Thailand. Serve this decadent shrimp on top a bed of mango sticky rice for one delicious meal.

Servings: 4 | **Preparation time:** time: 1 hour 20 minutes | **Cooking TIME:** 5 minutes

INGREDIENTS:

- 1-1/2 pounds uncooked jumbo shrimp, peeled and deveined
- 1/2 cup light coconut milk
- 1 tablespoon cilantro, chopped
- 4 teaspoons Tabasco Original Red Sauce
- 2 teaspoons soy sauce
- 1/4 cup freshly squeezed orange juice
- 1/4 cup freshly squeezed lime juice (from about 2 large limes)
- 3/4-pound pineapple, cut into 1-inch chunks
- Olive oil, for griddling

DIRECTIONS:

1. Combine the coconut milk, cilantro, Tabasco sauce, soy sauce, orange juice, lime juice. Add the shrimp and toss to coat.
2. Cover and place in the refrigerator to marinate for 1 hour.
3. Thread shrimp and pineapple onto metal skewers, alternating each.
4. Preheat griddle to medium heat.
5. Cook 5-6 minutes, flipping once, until shrimp turn opaque pink.
6. Serve immediately.

NUTRITION: Calories: 150, Sodium: 190mg, Dietary Fiber: 1.9g, Fat: 10.8g, Carbs: 14.9g, Protein: 1.5g.

Mexican Shrimp Tacos

Shrimp tacos are a great way to whip up a healthy dinner in no time for the whole family. These tacos are spiced to perfection and will definitely become a family favorite in no time!

Servings: 4 | **Preparation time:** Time: 10 minutes | **Cooking TIME:** 10 minutes

INGREDIENTS:

- 2 lbs. medium shrimp, peeled and deveined
- 8 flour tortillas, warmed
- 1 bag cabbage slaw
- 1 cup salsa
- 1 cup Mexican crema
- For marinade:
- 2 tablespoons olive oil
- 1 tablespoon chili powder
- 1 tablespoon cumin
- 1 tablespoon garlic powder
- 1 tablespoon fresh lime juice
- 1/4 teaspoon sea salt
- 1/8 teaspoon fresh ground pepper

DIRECTIONS:

1. Preheat a griddle to medium-high.
2. Combine oil marinade in a large sealable plastic bag. Add shrimp and toss coat; let marinate in the refrigerator for 30 minutes.
3. Cook shrimp for 3 minutes, on each side, until cooked through.
4. Transfer to a plate.
5. Lay two tortillas on each plate. Evenly divide the shrimp, cabbage slaw, salsa in the middle of each tortilla.
6. Drizzle with Mexican crema and serve.

NUTRITION: Calories: 400, Sodium: 92mg, Dietary Fiber: 4g, Fat: 14.7g, Carbs: 30.3g, Protein: 24g.

Bacon Wrapped Scallops

The delicate, sweet flavor of fresh sea scallops' pairs perfectly with the rich salty flavor of bacon. And best of all, you can **Prepare** this entire meal on your outdoor griddle.

Servings: 4 | **Preparation time:** time: 15 minutes | **Cooking TIME:** 4 minutes

INGREDIENTS:

- 12 large sea scallops, side muscle removed
- 8 slices of bacon
- 1 tablespoon vegetable oil
- 12 toothpicks

DIRECTIONS:

1. Heat your griddle to medium heat and cook the bacon until fat has rendered but bacon is still flexible. Remove bacon from the griddle and place on paper towels.
2. Raise griddle heat to medium-high.
3. Wrap each scallop with a half slice of bacon and skewer with a toothpick to keep the bacon in place.
4. Place the scallops on the griddle and cook for 90 seconds per side. They should be lightly browned on both sides.
5. Remove from the griddle and serve immediately.

NUTRITION: Calories: 315, Sodium: 1023mg, Dietary Fiber: 0g, Fat: 20g, Carbs: 2.7g, Protein: 29.2g.

Scallops with Lemony Salsa Verde

Brighten up your Griddle scallops with a citrus-infused Salsa Verde. Lemony Salsa Verde is the perfect complement to hearty scallops and delicious served alongside risotto or a gorgeous salad.

Servings: 2 | **Preparation time:** time: 10 minutes | **Cooking TIME:** 5 minutes

INGREDIENTS:

- 1 tablespoon olive oil, plus more for griddling
- 12 large sea scallops, side muscle removed
- Sea salt, for seasoning
- For the Lemony Salsa Verde:
- 1/2 lemon, with peel, seeded and chopped
- 5 tomatillos, peeled and pulsed in a blender
- 1 small shallot, finely chopped
- 1 garlic clove, finely chopped
- 1/4 cup olive oil
- 3/4 cup finely chopped fresh parsley
- 1/2 cup finely chopped fresh cilantro
- 1/4 cup chopped fresh chives
- 1/4 teaspoon sea salt
- 1/4 teaspoon black pepper

DIRECTIONS:

1. Toss Lemony Salsa ingredients in a small mixing bowl and set aside.
2. Preheat griddle for medium-high and brush with olive oil.
3. Toss scallops with 1 tablespoon olive oil on a baking sheet and season with salt.
4. Add scallops to griddle, turning once after 45 seconds to 1 minute. Cook an additional 1 minute before removing from the griddle.
5. Serve scallops topped with Lemony Salsa Verde.

NUTRITION: Calories: 267, Sodium: 541mg, Dietary Fiber: 3.1g, Fat: 9.6g, Carbs: 13.9g, Protein: 32.4g.

Griddle Oysters with Spiced Tequila Butter

Tequila infused butter is just the way to elevate oysters fresh off the griddle. A delicious appetizer, these oysters are also yummy served with a glass of Sauvignon Blanc or crisp lager and French fries.

Servings: 6 | **Preparation time:** time: 5 minutes | **Cooking TIME:** 25 minutes

INGREDIENTS:

- 3 dozen medium oysters, scrubbed and shucked
- Flakey sea salt, for serving
- For the butter:
- 1/4 teaspoon crushed red pepper
- 7 tablespoons unsalted butter
- 1/4 teaspoon chili oil
- 1 teaspoon dried oregano
- 2 tablespoons freshly squeezed lemon juice
- 2 tablespoons Tequila Blanco, like Espolon

DIRECTIONS:

1. Combine butter ingredients in a small mixing bowl until well-incorporated and set aside.
2. Preheat griddle to high.
3. Griddle the oysters about 1 to 2 minutes.
4. Sprinkle the oysters with salt flakes.
5. Warm the butter in a microwave for 30 seconds, and spoon the warm Tequila butter over the oysters and serve.

NUTRITION: Calories: 184, Sodium: 300mg, Dietary Fiber: 0.2g, Fat: 15g, Carbs: 3.8g, Protein: 0.2g.

Pop-Open Clams with Horseradish-Tabasco Sauce

These spicy clams are a great way to serve up some decadent seafood right at home. Best served with crusty Griddle bread, you'll love this delicious recipe as a starter or side to the perfect dinner.

Servings: 4 | **Preparation time:** time: 5 minutes | **Cooking TIME:** 10 minutes

INGREDIENTS:

- 2 dozen littleneck clams, scrubbed
- 4 tablespoons unsalted butter, softened
- 2 tablespoons horseradish, drained
- 1 tablespoon hot sauce, like Tabasco
- 1/4 teaspoon lemon zest, finely grated
- 1 tablespoon fresh lemon juice
- 1/4 teaspoon smoked paprika
- Sea salt

DIRECTIONS:

1. Preheat the griddle to high.
2. Blend the butter with the horseradish, hot sauce, lemon zest, lemon juice, paprika, and pinch of salt.
3. Arrange the clams over high heat and griddle until they pop open, about 25 seconds.
4. Carefully turn the clams over using tongs, so the meat side is down.
5. Griddle for about 20 seconds longer, until the clam juices start to simmer.
6. Transfer the clams to a serving bowl.
7. Top each with about 1/2 teaspoon of the sauce and serve.

NUTRITION: Calories: 191, Sodium: 382mg, Dietary Fiber: 0.3g, Fat: 12.7g, Carbs: 4g, Protein: 14.8g.

Spicy Griddle Squid

Spice things up with this yummy recipe and serve up some squid at your next dinner party. The perfect appetizer, this is best served on its own or as a decadent appetizer on a bed of leafy greens.

Servings: 4 | **Preparation time:** time: 5 minutes | **Cooking TIME:** 5 minutes

INGREDIENTS:

- 1-1/2 lbs. Squid, **Prepared**
- Olive oil
- For the marinade:
- 2 cloves garlic cloves, minced
- 1/2 teaspoon ginger, minced
- 3 tablespoons gochujang
- 3 tablespoons corn syrup
- 1 teaspoon yellow mustard
- 1 teaspoon soy sauce
- 2 teaspoons sesame oil
- 1 teaspoon sesame seeds
- 2 green onions, chopped

DIRECTIONS:

1. Preheat griddle to medium high heat and brush with olive oil.
2. Add the squid and tentacles to the griddle and cook for 1 minute until the bottom looks firm and opaque.
3. Turn them over and cook for another minute; straighten out the body with tongs if it curls.
4. Baste with sauce on top of the squid and cook 2 additional minutes.
5. Flip and baste the other side, cook 1 minute until the sauce evaporates and the squid turns red and shiny.

NUTRITION: Calories: 292, Sodium: 466mg, Dietary Fiber: 2.7g, Fat: 8.6g, Carbs: 25.1g, Protein: 27.8g.

VEGETABLE & SIDE DISHES

Stir Fry Mushrooms

Preparation Time: 10 minutes
Cooking Time: 10 minutes
Servings: 2

INGREDIENTS:

- 10 oz mushrooms, sliced
- 1/4 cup olive oil
- 1 tbsp garlic, minced
- 1/4 tsp dried thyme
- Pepper
- Salt

DIRECTIONS:

1. Preheat the griddle to high heat.
2. Add 2 tablespoons of oil to the hot griddle top.
3. Add mushrooms, garlic, thyme, pepper, and salt and sauté mushrooms until tender.
4. Drizzle remaining oil and serve.

NUTRITION: Calories 253 Fat 25.6 g Carbohydrates 6.2 g Sugar 2.5 g Protein 4.7 g Cholesterol 0 mg

Stir Fry Vegetables

Preparation Time: 10 minutes
Cooking Time: 20 minutes
Servings: 4

INGREDIENTS:

- 2 medium potatoes, cut into small pieces
- 3 medium carrots, peeled and cut into small pieces
- 1/4 cup olive oil
- 1 small rutabaga, peeled and cut into small pieces
- 2 medium parsnips, peeled and cut into small pieces
- Pepper
- Salt

DIRECTIONS:

1. Preheat the griddle to high heat.
2. In a large bowl, toss vegetables with olive oil.
3. Transfer vegetables onto the hot griddle top and stir fry until vegetables are tender.
4. Serve and enjoy.

NUTRITION: Calories 218 Fat 12.8 g Carbohydrates 25.2 g Sugar 6.2 g Protein 2.8 g Cholesterol 0 mg

Easy Fried Rice

Preparation Time: 10 minutes
Cooking Time: 10 minutes
Servings: 2

INGREDIENTS:

- 4 cups rice, cooked
- 2 large eggs
- 2 tbsp green onion, sliced
- 2 tbsp olive oil
- 1 tsp salt

DIRECTIONS:

1. In a bowl, whisk eggs and set aside.
2. Preheat the griddle to high heat.
3. Spray griddle top with cooking spray.
4. Add cooked rice on hot griddle top and fry until rice separate from each other.
5. Push rice to one side of the griddle top. Add oil to the griddle and pour beaten egg.
6. Add salt and mix egg quickly with rice and cook until rice grains are covered by egg.
7. Add green onion and stir fry for 2 minutes.
8. Serve and enjoy.

NUTRITION: Calories 557 Fat 19.8 g Carbohydrates 79.6 g Sugar 0.7 g Protein 14 g Cholesterol 186 mg

Healthy Zucchini Noodles

Preparation Time: 10 minutes
Cooking Time: 10 minutes
Servings: 4

INGREDIENTS:

- 4 small zucchinis, spiralized
- 1 tbsp soy sauce
- 2 onions, spiralized
- 2 tbsp olive oil
- 1 tbsp sesame seeds
- 2 tbsp teriyaki sauce

DIRECTIONS:

1. Preheat the griddle to high heat.
2. Add oil to the hot griddle top.
3. Add onion and sauté for 4-5 minutes.
4. Add zucchini noodles and cook for 2 minutes.
5. Add sesame seeds, teriyaki sauce, and soy sauce and cook for 4-5 minutes.
6. Serve and enjoy.

NUTRITION: Calories 124 Fat 8.4 g Carbohydrates 11.3 g Sugar 5.7 g Protein 3.2 g Cholesterol 0 mg

Easy Seared Green Beans

Preparation Time: 10 minutes
Cooking Time: 10 minutes
Servings: 6

INGREDIENTS:

- 1 1/2 lbs. green beans, trimmed
- 1 1/2 tbsp rice vinegar
- 3 tbsp soy sauce
- 1 1/2 tbsp sesame oil
- 2 tbsp sesame seeds, toasted
- 1 1/2 tbsp brown sugar
- 1/4 tsp black pepper

DIRECTIONS:

1. Cook green beans in boiling water for 3 minutes and drain well.
2. Transfer green beans to chilled ice water and drain again. Pat dry green beans.
3. Preheat the griddle to high heat.
4. Add oil to the hot griddle top.
5. Add green beans and stir fry for 2 minutes.
6. Add soy sauce, brown sugar, vinegar, and pepper and stir fry for 2 minutes more.
7. Add sesame seeds and toss well to coat.
8. Serve and enjoy.

NUTRITION: Calories 100 Fat 5 g Carbohydrates 11.7 g Sugar 3.9 g Protein 3.1 g Cholesterol 0 mg

Stir Fry Bok Choy

Preparation Time: 10 minutes
Cooking Time: 5 minutes
Servings: 4

INGREDIENTS:

- 2 heads bok choy, trimmed and cut crosswise
- 1 tsp sesame oil
- 2 tsp soy sauce
- 2 tbsp water
- 1 tbsp butter
- 1 tbsp peanut oil
- 1 tbsp oyster sauce
- 1/2 tsp salt

DIRECTIONS:

1. In a small bowl, mix together soy sauce, oyster sauce, sesame oil, and water and set aside.
2. Preheat the griddle to high heat.
3. Add oil to the hot griddle top.
4. Add bok choy and salt and stir fry for 2 minutes.
5. Add butter and soy sauce mixture and stir fry for 1-2 minutes.
6. Serve and enjoy.

NUTRITION: Calories 122 Fat 8.2 g Carbohydrates 9.5 g Sugar 5 g Protein 6.5 g Cholesterol 8 mg

Sautéed Vegetables

Preparation Time: 10 minutes
Cooking Time: 5 minutes
Servings: 4

INGREDIENTS:

- 2 medium zucchinis, cut into matchsticks
- 2 tbsp coconut oil
- 2 tsp garlic, minced
- 1 tbsp honey
- 3 tbsp soy sauce
- 1 tsp sesame seeds
- 2 cups carrots, cut into matchsticks
- 2 cups snow peas

DIRECTIONS:

1. In a small bowl, mix together soy sauce, garlic, and honey and set aside.
2. Preheat the griddle to high heat.
3. Add oil to the hot griddle top.
4. Add carrots, snow peas, and zucchini, and sauté for 1-2 minutes.
5. Add soy sauce mixture and stir fry for 1 minute.
6. Garnish with sesame seeds and serve.

NUTRITION: Calories 160 Fat 7.5 g Carbohydrates 20.2 g Sugar 12.1 g Protein 5.3 g Cholesterol 0 mg

Stir Fry Cabbage

Preparation Time: 10 minutes
Cooking Time: 5 minutes
Servings: 4

INGREDIENTS:

- 1 cabbage head, tear cabbage leaves, washed and drained
- 2 green onion, sliced
- 1 tbsp ginger, minced
- 2 garlic cloves, minced
- 1 tbsp soy sauce
- 1/2 tbsp vinegar
- 4 dried chilies
- 2 tbsp olive oil
- 1/2 tsp salt

DIRECTIONS:

1. Preheat the griddle to high heat.
2. Add oil to the hot griddle top.
3. Add ginger, garlic, and green onion and sauté for 2-3 minutes.
4. Add dried chilies and sauté for 30 seconds.
5. Add cabbage, vinegar, soy sauce, and salt and stir fry for 1-2 minutes over high heat until cabbage wilted.
6. Serve and enjoy.

NUTRITION: Calories 115 Fat 7.3 g Carbohydrates 12.7 g Sugar 6 g Protein 2.9 g Cholesterol 0 mg

Pineapple Fried Rice

Preparation Time: 10 minutes
Cooking Time: 10 minutes
Servings: 4

INGREDIENTS:

- 3 cups cooked brown rice
- 1/2 cup frozen corn
- 2 carrots, peeled and grated
- 1 onion, diced
- 2 garlic cloves, minced
- 2 tbsp olive oil
- 1/2 tsp ginger powder
- 1 tbsp sesame oil
- 3 tbsp soy sauce
- 1/4 cup green onion, sliced
- 1/2 cup ham, diced
- 2 cups pineapple, diced
- 1/2 cup frozen peas

DIRECTIONS:

1. In a small bowl, whisk soy sauce, ginger powder, and sesame oil and set aside.
2. Preheat the griddle to high heat.
3. Add oil to the hot griddle top.
4. Add onion and garlic and sauté for 3-4 minutes.
5. Add corn, carrots, and peas and stir constantly for 3-4 minutes.
6. Stir in cooked rice, green onions, ham, pineapple, and soy sauce mixture and stir continuously for 2-3 minutes.
7. Serve and enjoy.

NUTRITION: Calories 375 Fat 13.3 g Carbohydrates 57.6 g Sugar 12.7 g Protein 9.4 g Cholesterol 10 mg

Italian Zucchini Slices

Preparation Time: 10 minutes
Cooking Time: 5 minutes
Servings: 4

INGREDIENTS:

- 2 zucchinis, cut into 1/2-inch-thick slices
- 1 tsp Italian seasoning
- 2 garlic cloves, minced
- 1/4 cup butter, melted
- 1 1/2 tbsp fresh parsley, chopped
- 1 tbsp fresh lemon juice
- Pepper
- Salt

DIRECTIONS:

1. In a small bowl, mix melted butter, lemon juice, Italian seasoning, garlic, pepper, and salt.
2. Brush zucchini slices with melted butter mixture.
3. Preheat the griddle to high heat.
4. Place zucchini slices on the griddle top and cook for 2 minutes per side.
5. Transfer zucchini slices on serving plate and garnish with parsley.
6. Serve and enjoy.

NUTRITION: Calories 125 Fat 12 g Carbohydrates 4.1 g Sugar 1.9 g Protein 1.5 g Cholesterol 31 mg

GAME RECIPES

Flavorful Cornish Game Hen

Preparation Time: 10 minutes
Cooking Time: 60 minutes
Serve: 2

INGREDIENTS:
- 1 Cornish game hen
- 1/2 tbsp olive oil
- 1/4 tbsp poultry seasoning

DIRECTIONS:
1. Brush hen with oil and rub with poultry seasoning.
2. Preheat the griddle to high heat.
3. Spray griddle top with cooking spray.
4. Place hen on hot griddle top and cook from all the sides until brown.
5. Cover hen with lid or pan and cook for 60 minutes or until the internal temperature of hen reaches 180 F.
6. Slice and serve.

NUTRITIONAL: Value (Amount per Serving): Calories 366 Fat 26.9 g Carbohydrates 0.3 g Sugar 0 g Protein 28 g Cholesterol 168 mg

Flavorful Marinated Cornish Hen

Preparation Time: 10 minutes
Cooking Time: 60 minutes
Serve: 2

INGREDIENTS:
- 1 Cornish hen
- 1 cup cold water
- 16 oz apple juice
- 1/8 cup brown sugar
- 1 cinnamon stick
- 1 cup hot water
- 1/4 cup kosher salt

DIRECTIONS:
1. Add cinnamon, hot water, cold water, apple juice, brown sugar, and salt into the large pot and stir until sugar is dissolved.
2. Add hen in the brine and place in the refrigerator for 4 hours.
3. Preheat the griddle to high heat.
4. Spray griddle top with cooking spray.
5. Remove hens from brine and place on hot griddle top and cook for 60 minutes or until internal temperature reaches 160 F.
6. Slice and serve.

NUTRITIONAL: Value (Amount per Serving): Calories 938 Fat 9.5 g Carbohydrates 232 g Sugar 200 g Protein 10 g Cholesterol 51 mg

Montreal Seasoned Spatchcocked Hens

Preparation Time: 10 minutes

Cooking Time: 60 minutes

Serve: 2

INGREDIENTS:

- 1 Cornish hen
- 1 tbsp olive oil
- 1 tbsp Montreal chicken seasoning

DIRECTIONS:

1. Cut the backbone of hens and flatten the breastplate.
2. Brush hen with oil and rub with Montreal chicken seasoning.
3. Wrap hens in plastic wrap and place in the refrigerator for 4 hours.
4. Preheat the griddle to high heat.
5. Spray griddle top with cooking spray.
6. Place marinated hen on hot griddle top and cook for 60 minutes or until internal temperature reaches 180 F.
7. Serve and enjoy.

NUTRITIONAL: Value (Amount per Serving): Calories 228 Fat 18 g Carbohydrates 0 g Sugar 0 g Protein 14 g Cholesterol 85 mg

Rosemary Hen

Preparation Time: 10 minutes

Cooking Time: 60 minutes

Serve: 2

INGREDIENTS:

- 1 Cornish game hen
- 1 tbsp butter, melted
- 1/2 tbsp rosemary, minced
- 1 tsp chicken rub

DIRECTIONS:

1. Brush hens with melted butter.
2. Mix together rosemary and chicken rub.
3. Rub hen with rosemary and chicken rub mixture.
4. Preheat the griddle to high heat.
5. Spray griddle top with cooking spray.
6. Place hen on hot griddle top and cook for 60 minutes or until internal temperature reaches 165 F.
7. Serve and enjoy.

NUTRITIONAL: Value (Amount per Serving): Calories 221 Fat 17 g Carbohydrates 0.5 g Sugar 0 g Protein 14.5 g Cholesterol 100 mg

BBQ Hen

Preparation Time: 10 minutes
Cooking Time: 1 hour 30 minutes
Serve: 8

INGREDIENTS:

* 1 Cornish hen
* 2 tbsp BBQ rub

DIRECTIONS:

1. Preheat the griddle to high heat.
2. Spray griddle top with cooking spray.
3. Coat hens with BBQ rub and place on hot griddle top and cook for 1 1/2 hours or until the internal temperature of hens reach 165 F.
4. Slice and serve.

NUTRITIONAL: Value (Amount per Serving): Calories 168 Fat 11 g Carbohydrates 0 g Sugar 0 g Protein 14 g Cholesterol 85 mg

Honey Garlic Cornish Hen

Preparation Time: 10 minutes
Cooking Time: 60 minutes
Serve: 2

INGREDIENTS:

* 1 Cornish hen
* 2 garlic cloves, minced
* 1/8 cup honey
* 1/4 cup soy sauce
* 3/4 cup warm water
* 1 tbsp cornstarch
* 1/4 cup brown sugar

DIRECTIONS:

1. Mix together soy sauce, warm water, brown sugar, garlic, cornstarch, and honey.
2. Place Cornish hen in baking dish and season with pepper and salt.
3. Pour marinade over hen and place in the refrigerator for 10 hours.
4. Preheat the griddle to high heat.
5. Spray griddle top with cooking spray.
6. Place marinated hen on hot griddle top and cook for 60 minutes or until internal temperature reaches 165 F.
7. Serve and enjoy.

NUTRITIONAL: Value (Amount per Serving): Calories 338 Fat 11.8 g Carbohydrates 42.3 g Sugar 35.6 g Protein 16.6 g Cholesterol 85 mg

Sage Thyme Cornish Hen

Preparation Time: 10 minutes
Cooking Time: 60 minutes
Serve: 2

INGREDIENTS:

- 1 Cornish hen
- 1/2 tbsp paprika
- 1/4 tsp pepper
- 1/4 tsp sage
- 1/2 tsp thyme
- 1/2 tbsp onion powder

DIRECTIONS:

1. In a small bowl, mix together paprika, onion powder, thyme, sage, and pepper.
2. Rub hen with paprika mixture.
3. Preheat the griddle to high heat.
4. Spray griddle top with cooking spray.
5. Place hen on hot griddle top and cook for 60 minutes or until internal temperature reaches 185 F.
6. Serve and enjoy.

NUTRITIONAL Value (Amount per Serving): Calories 180 Fat 12 g Carbohydrates 2.7 g Sugar 0.8 g Protein 14.9 g Cholesterol 85 mg

Asian Cornish Hen

Preparation Time: 10 minutes
Cooking Time: 60 minutes
Serve: 2

INGREDIENTS:

- 1 Cornish hen
- 1 1/2 tsp Chinese five-spice powder
- 1 1/2 tsp rice wine
- 1/2 tsp pepper
- 2 cups of water
- 3 tbsp soy sauce
- 2 tbsp sugar
- Salt

DIRECTIONS:

1. In a large bowl, mix together water, soy sauce, sugar, rice wine, five-spice, pepper, and salt.
2. Place Cornish hen in the bowl and place in the refrigerator for overnight.
3. Preheat the griddle to high heat.
4. Spray griddle top with cooking spray.
5. Remove Cornish hen from marinade and place on hot griddle top and cook for 60 minutes or until internal temperature reaches 185 F.
6. Slice and serve.

NUTRITIONAL: Value (Amount per Serving): Calories 233 Fat 11.8 g Carbohydrates 15.9 g Sugar 13.4 g Protein 15.9 g Cholesterol 85 mg

Orange Cornish Hen

Preparation Time: 10 minutes
Cooking Time: 60 minutes
Serve: 2

INGREDIENTS:

- 1 Cornish hen
- 1/4 onion, cut into chunks
- 1/4 orange cut into wedges
- 2 garlic cloves
- 4 fresh sage leaves
- 1 1/2 fresh rosemary sprigs
- For glaze:
- 2-star anise
- 1 tbsp honey
- 1 cup orange juice
- 1/4 fresh orange, sliced
- 1/2 orange zest
- 1.5 oz Grand Marnier
- 1/2 cinnamon stick

DIRECTIONS:

1. Stuff hen with orange wedges, garlic, onions, and herbs. Season with pepper and salt.
2. Preheat the griddle to high heat.
3. Spray griddle top with cooking spray.
4. Place hen on hot griddle top and cook for 60 minutes or until the internal temperature of hens reaches 165 F.
5. Meanwhile, in a saucepan heat, all glaze ingredients until reduce by half over medium-high heat.
6. Brush hen with glaze.
7. Slice and serve.

NUTRITIONAL: Value (Amount per Serving): Calories 351 Fat 12.1 g Carbohydrates 29.2 g Sugar 40.9 g Protein 16 g Cholesterol 85 mg

Rosemary Butter Cornish Hens

Preparation Time: 10 minutes
Cooking Time: 60 minutes
Serve: 2

INGREDIENTS:

- 1 Cornish hen, rinse and pat dry with paper towels
- 1 tbsp butter, melted
- 1 rosemary sprigs
- 1 tsp poultry seasoning

DIRECTIONS:

1. Stuff rosemary sprigs into the hen cavity.
2. Brush hen with melted butter and season with poultry seasoning.
3. Preheat the griddle to high heat.
4. Spray griddle top with cooking spray.
5. Place hen on hot griddle top and cook for 60 minutes or until the internal temperature of hens reaches 165 F.
6. Slice and serve.

NUTRITIONAL: Value (Amount per Serving): Calories 127 Fat 8 g Carbohydrates 0.5 g Sugar 0 g Protein 13 g Cholesterol 74 mg

APPETIZERS AND SIDES RECIPES

Smashed Potato Casserole

Preparation Time: 30 minutes
Cooking Time: 45 - 60 minutes
Servings: 8

INGREDIENTS:

- 1 small red onion, thinly sliced
- 1 small green bell pepper, thinly sliced
- 1 small red bell pepper, thinly sliced
- 1 small yellow bell pepper, thinly sliced
- 3 cups mashed potatoes
- 8 - 10 bacon slices
- ¼ cup bacon grease or salted butter (½ stick)
- ¾ cup sour cream
- 1 ½ teaspoons barbecue rub
- 3 cups shredded sharp cheddar cheese (divided)
- 4 cups hash brown potatoes (frozen)
- Intolerances:
- Gluten-Free
- Egg-Free

DIRECTIONS:

1. Get that bacon cooking over medium heat in a large griddle. Cook till nice and crisp. Aim for 5 minutes on both sides. Then set aside your bacon.

2. Pour the bacon grease into a glass container and set aside.

3. Using the same griddle, warm up the butter or bacon grease over medium heat. When warm enough, sauté bell peppers and red onions. You're aiming for al dente. When done, set it all aside.

4. Grab a casserole dish, preferably one that is 9 by 11 inches. Spray with some nonstick cooking spray, then spread the mashed potatoes out, covering the entire bottom of the dish.

5. Add the sour cream to the next layer over the potatoes. When you're done, season it with some of the barbecue rub.

6. Create a new layer with the sautéed veggies over the potatoes, leaving the butter or grease in the pan.

7. Sprinkle your sharp cheddar cheese—just 1½ of the cups. Then add the frozen hash brown potatoes.

8. Scoop out the rest of the bacon grease or butter from the sautéed veggies, all over the hash browns, and then top it all off with some delicious crumbled bacon bits.

9. Add the rest of the sharp cheddar cheese (1½ cups) over the whole thing, and then use some aluminum foil to cover the casserole dish.

10. Set up your griddle for indirect cooking. Preheat to 350ºF.

11. Let the whole thing bake for 45 - 60 minutes. Ideally, you want the cheese to bubble.

12. Take it out and let it sit for about 10 minutes.

13. Serve!

NUTRITION: Calories: 232 Fat: 2g Carbs: 48g Protein: 9g

Atomic Buffalo Turds

Preparation Time: 30 minutes

Cooking Time: 1 hour and 30 minutes

Servings: 10

INGREDIENTS:

- 8 ounces regular cream cheese (room temp)
- 10 jalapeno peppers (medium)
- ¾ cup cheddar cheese blend and shredded Monterey Jack (not necessary)
- 1 teaspoon smoked paprika
- 1 teaspoon garlic powder
- ½ teaspoon red pepper flakes (not necessary)
- Little Smokies sausages (20)
- 10 bacon strips, thinly sliced and halved
- Intolerances:
- Egg-Free

DIRECTIONS:

1. Wash the jalapenos, then slice them up along the length. Get a spoon, or a paring knife if you prefer, and use that to take out the seeds and the veins.
2. Place the scooped-out jalapenos on a veggie griddling tray and put it all aside.
3. Get a small bowl and mix the shredded cheese, cream cheese, paprika, cayenne pepper, garlic powder, and red pepper flakes. Mix them thoroughly.
4. Get your jalapenos which you've hollowed out, and then stuff them with the cream cheese mix.
5. Get your little Smokies sausage, and then put it right onto each of the cheese stuffed jalapenos.
6. Grab some of the thinly sliced and halved bacon strips and wrap them around each of the stuffed jalapenos and their sausage.
7. Grab some toothpicks. Use them to keep the bacon nicely secured to the sausage.
8. Set up your griddle so it's ready for indirect cooking. Get it preheated to 250ºF.
9. Put your jalapeno peppers in and smoke them at 250ºF for anywhere from 90 minutes to 120 minutes. You want to keep it going until the bacon is nice and crispy.
10. Take out the atomic buffalo turds, and then let them rest for about 5 minutes.
11. Serve!

NUTRITION: Calories: 198 Fat: 17g Cholesterol: 48mg Carbs: 3g Protein: 8g

Brisket Baked Beans

Preparation Time: 20 minutes
Cooking Time: 1 hour and 30 minutes
Servings: 10

INGREDIENTS:

- 1 green bell pepper (medium, diced)
- 1 red bell pepper (medium, diced)
- 1 yellow onion (large, diced)
- 2 - 6 jalapeno peppers (diced)
- 2 tablespoons olive oil (extra-virgin)
- 3 cups brisket flat (chopped)
- 1 can baked beans (28 ounces)
- 1 can red kidney beans (1 4ounces, rinsed, drained)
- 1 cup barbecue sauce
- ½ cup brown sugar (packed)
- 2 teaspoons mustard (ground)
- 3 cloves of garlic (chopped)
- 1 ½ teaspoon black pepper
- 1 ½ teaspoon kosher salt
- Intolerances:
- Gluten-Free
- Egg-Free
- Lactose-Free

DIRECTIONS:

1. Put a griddle on the fire, on medium heat. Warm up your olive oil. Toss in the diced jalapenos, peppers, and onions. Stir every now and then for 8 minutes.
2. Grab a 4-quart casserole dish. Now, in your dish, mix in the pork and beans, kidney beans, baked beans, chopped brisket, cooked peppers and onions, brown sugar, barbecue sauce, garlic, mustard, salt, and black pepper.
3. Set up your griddle so it's ready for indirect cooking.
4. Preheat your griddle to 325ºF.
5. Cook your brisket beans on the griddle, for 90 minutes to 120 minutes. Keep it uncovered as you cook. When it's ready, you'll know, because the beans will get thicker and will have bubbles as well.
6. Rest the food for 15 minutes, before you finally move on to step number 5.
7. Serve!

NUTRITION: Calories: 200 Fat: 2g Cholesterol: 10mg Carbs: 35g Protein: 9g

Twice-Baked Spaghetti Squash

Preparation Time: 15 minutes

Cooking Time: 1 hour

Servings: 2

INGREDIENTS:

- 1 spaghetti squash (medium)
- 1 tablespoon olive oil (extra virgin)
- 1 teaspoon salt
- ½ teaspoon pepper
- ½ cup Parmesan cheese (grated, divided)
- ½ cup mozzarella cheese (shredded, divided)
- Intolerances:
- Egg-Free

DIRECTIONS:

1. Cut the squash along the length in half. Make sure you're using a knife that's large enough, and sharp enough. Once you're done, take out the pulp and the seeds from each half with a spoon.

2. Rub the insides of each half of the squash with some olive oil. When you're done with that, sprinkle the salt and pepper.

3. Set up your griddle for indirect cooking.

4. Preheat your griddle to 375ºF.

5. Put each half of the squash on the griddle. Make sure they're both facing upwards on the griddle grates, which should be nice and hot.

6. Bake for 45 minutes, keeping it on the griddle until the internal temperature of the squash hits 170ºF. You'll know you're done when you find it easy to pierce the squash with a fork.

7. Move the squash to your cutting board. Let it sit there for 10 minutes, so it can cool a bit.

8. Turn up the temp on your griddle to 425ºF.

9. Use a fork to remove the flesh from the squash in strands by raking it back and forth. Do be careful, because you want the shells to remain intact. The strands you rake off should look like spaghetti, if you're doing it right.

10. Put the spaghetti squash strands in a large bowl, and then add in half of your mozzarella and half of your Parmesan cheeses. Combine them by stirring.

11. Take the mix, and stuff it into the squash shells. When you're done, sprinkle them with the rest of the Parmesan and mozzarella cheeses.

12. Optional: You can top these with some bacon bits, if you like.

13. Allow the stuffed spaghetti squash shells you've now stuffed to bake at 435ºF for 15 minutes, or however long it takes the cheese to go brown.

14. Serve and enjoy.

NUTRITION: Calories: 214 Fat: 3g Cholesterol: 17mg Carbs: 27g Protein: 16g

Bacon-Wrapped Asparagus

Preparation Time: 15 minutes
Cooking Time: 25 - 30 minutes
Servings: 6

INGREDIENTS:

- 15 - 20 spears of fresh asparagus (1 pound)
- Olive oil (extra virgin)
- 5 slices bacon (thinly sliced)
- 1 teaspoon salt and pepper (or your preferred rub)
- intolerances:
- Gluten-Free
- Egg-Free
- Lactose-Free

DIRECTIONS:

1. Break off the ends of the asparagus, then trim it all so they're down to the same length.
2. Separate the asparagus into bundles—3 spears per bundle. Then spritz them with some olive oil.
3. Use a piece of bacon to wrap up each bundle. When you're done, lightly dust the wrapped bundle with some salt and pepper to taste, or your preferred rub.
4. Set up your griddle so that it's ready for indirect cooking.
5. Put some fiberglass mats on your grates. Make sure they're the fiberglass kind. This will keep your asparagus from getting stuck on your griddle gates.
6. Preheat your griddle to 400°F.
7. Griddle the wraps for 25 minutes to 30 minutes, tops. The goal is to get your asparagus looking nice and tender, and the bacon deliciously crispy.

NUTRITION: Calories: 71 Fat: 3g Carbs: 1g Protein: 6g

Garlic Parmesan Wedges

Preparation Time: 15 minutes
Cooking Time: 35 minutes
Servings: 3

INGREDIENTS:

- 3 russet potatoes (large)
- 2 teaspoons of garlic powder
- ¾ teaspoon black pepper
- 1 ½ teaspoons of salt
- ¾ cup Parmesan cheese (grated)
- 3 tablespoons fresh cilantro (chopped, optional. You can replace this with flat-leaf parsley)
- ½ cup blue cheese (per serving, as optional dip. Can be replaced with ranch dressing)
- Intolerances:
- Gluten-Free
- Egg-Free

DIRECTIONS:

1. Use some cold water to scrub your potatoes as gently as you can with a veggie brush. When done, let them dry.
2. Slice your potatoes along the length in half. Cut each half into a third.
3. Get all the extra moisture off your potato by wiping it all away with a paper towel. If you don't do this, then you're not going to have crispy wedges!
4. In a large bowl, throw in your potato wedges, some olive oil, garlic powder, salt, garlic, and pepper, and then toss them with your hands, lightly. You want to make sure the spices and oil get on every wedge.
5. Place your wedges on a nonstick tray, or pan, or basked. The single layer kind. Make sure it's at least 15 x 12 inches.
6. Set up your griddle so it's ready for indirect cooking.
7. Preheat your griddle to 425ºF.
8. Set the tray upon your preheated griddle. Roast the wedges for 15 minutes before you flip them. Once you turn them, roast them for another 15 minutes, or 20 tops. The outside should be a nice, crispy, golden brown.
9. Sprinkle your wedges generously with the Parmesan cheese. When you're done, garnish it with some parsley, or cilantro, if you like. Serve these bad boys up with some ranch dressing, or some blue cheese, or just eat them that way!

NUTRITION: Calories: 194 Fat: 5g Cholesterol: 5mg Carbs: 32g Protein: 5g

Smoked Moink Ball Skewers

Preparation Time: 30 minutes

Cooking Time: 1 hour and 15 minutes

Servings: 6

INGREDIENTS:

- ½ pound pork sausage (ground)
- ½ pound ground beef (80% lean)
- 1 egg (large)
- ½ cup red onions (minced)
- ½ cup Parmesan cheese (grated)
- ½ cup Italian breadcrumbs
- ¼ cup parsley (finely chopped)
- ¼ cup milk (whole)
- 2 garlic cloves (minced) or 1 teaspoon garlic (crushed)
- 1 teaspoon oregano
- ½ teaspoon kosher salt
- ½ teaspoon black pepper
- ¼ cup barbecue sauce
- ½ pound bacon slices (thinly sliced, halved)
- Intolerances:
- Egg-Free

DIRECTIONS:

1.   Mix up the ground pork sausage, ground beef, breadcrumbs, onion, egg, parsley, Parmesan cheese, garlic, milk, oregano, salt, and pepper in a large bowl. Whatever you do, don't overwork your meat.

2.   Make meatballs of 1½ ounces each. They should be about 1½ in width. Put them on your Teflon-coated fiberglass mat.

3.   Wrap up each meatball in half a slice of your thinly sliced bacon.

4.   Spear your moink balls, three to a skewer.

5.   Set up your griddle so that it's nice and ready for indirect cooking.

6.   Preheat your griddle to 225ºF,

7.   Smoke the skewered moink balls for half an hour.

8.   Turn up the temperature to 350ºF, and keep it that way until the internal temperature of your skewered moink balls hits 175ºF, which should take about 40 to 45 minutes, max.

9.   When the bacon gets nice and crispy, brush your moink balls with whatever barbecue sauce you like. Ideally, you should do this in the last five minutes of your cook time.

10. Serve the moink ball skewers while they're hot.

NUTRITION: Calories: 314 Fat: 28g Protein: 15g

Bacon Cheddar Slider

Preparation Time: 30 minutes

Cooking Time: 15 minutes

Servings: 2

INGREDIENTS:

- 1-pound ground beef (80% lean)
- 1/2 teaspoon of garlic salt
- 1/2 teaspoon salt
- 1/2 teaspoon of garlic
- 1/2 teaspoon onion
- 1/2 teaspoon black pepper
- 6 bacon slices, cut in half
- 1/2 Cup mayonnaise
- 2 teaspoons of creamy wasabi (optional)
- 6 (1 oz) sliced sharp cheddar cheese, cut in half (optional)
- Sliced red onion
- 1/2 Cup sliced kosher dill pickles
- 12 mini breads sliced horizontally
- Ketchup
- Intolerances:
- Egg-Free

DIRECTIONS:

1. Place ground beef, garlic salt, seasoned salt, garlic powder, onion powder and black hupe pepper in a medium bowl.

2. Divide the meat mixture into 12 equal parts, shape into small thin round patties (about 2 ounces each) and save.

3. Cook the bacon on medium heat over medium heat for 5-8 minutes until crunchy. Set aside.

4. To make the sauce, mix the mayonnaise and horseradish in a small bowl, if used.

5. Preheat griddle to 350°F. Griddle surface should be approximately 400°F.

6. Spray a cooking spray on the griddle cooking surface for best non-stick results.

7. Griddle the putty for 3-4 minutes each until the internal temperature reaches 160°F.

8. If necessary, place a sharp cheddar cheese slice on each patty while the patty is on the griddle or after the patty is removed from the griddle.

9. Place a small amount of mayonnaise mixture, a slice of red onion, and a hamburger pate in the lower half of each roll. Pickled slices, bacon and ketchup.

NUTRITION: Calories: 160 Fat: 11g Carbs: 20g Protein: 10g

Mushrooms Stuffed with Crab Meat

Preparation Time: 20 minutes
Cooking Time: 30 – 45 minutes
Servings: 6

INGREDIENTS:

- 6 medium-sized portobello mushrooms
- Extra virgin olive oil
- 1/3 Grated parmesan cheese cup
- Club Beat Staffing:
- 8 oz fresh crab meat or canned or imitation crab meat
- 2 tablespoons extra virgin olive oil
- 1/3 Chopped celery
- Chopped red peppers
- 1/2 cup chopped green onion
- 1/2 cup Italian breadcrumbs
- 1/2 Cup mayonnaise
- 8 oz cream cheese at room temperature
- 1/2 teaspoon of garlic
- 1 tablespoon dried parsley
- Grated parmesan cheese cup
- 1 1 teaspoon of Old Bay seasoning
- 1/4 teaspoon of kosher salt
- 1/4 teaspoon black pepper
- Intolerances:
- Egg-Free

DIRECTIONS:

1. Clean the mushroom cap with a damp paper towel. Cut off the stem and save it.
2. Remove the brown gills from the bottom of the mushroom cap with a spoon and discard.
3. **Prepare** crab meat stuffing. If you are using canned crab meat, drain, rinse, and remove shellfish.
4. Heat the olive oil in a frying pan over medium high heat. Add celery, peppers and green onions and fry for 5 minutes. Set aside for cooling.
5. Gently pour the chilled sautéed vegetables and the remaining ingredients into a large bowl.
6. Cover and refrigerate crab meat stuffing until ready to use.
7. Put the crab mixture in each mushroom cap and make a mound in the center.
8. Sprinkle extra virgin olive oil and sprinkle parmesan cheese on each stuffed mushroom cap. Put the mushrooms in a 10 x 15-inch baking dish.
9. Use the griddle to indirect heating and preheat to 375°F.
10. Bake for 30-45 minutes until the filling becomes hot (165ºF as measured by an instant-read digital thermometer) and the mushrooms begin to release juice.

NUTRITION: Calories: 60 Fat: 4g Cholesterol: 20mg Carbs: 2g Protein: 2g

Parmesan Tomatoes

Preparation Time: 110 minutes

Cooking Time: 20 minutes

Servings: 6

INGREDIENTS:

- 9 halved Tomatoes
- 1 cup grated Parmesan cheese
- 1/2 tsp. Ground black pepper
- 1/4 tsp. Onion powder
- 1 tbsp. Dried rosemary
- 2 tbsps. Olive oil
- 5 minced Garlic cloves
- 1 tsp. Kosher salt
- Intolerances:
- Gluten-Free
- Egg-Free

DIRECTIONS:

1. Heat a griddle to medium-low heat and oil grates.
2. Place tomatoes halves cut side down, onto the griddle and cook for 5-7 minutes.
3. Heat olive oil in a pan over a medium heat. Add garlic, rosemary, black pepper, onion powder, and salt and cook for 3-5 minutes.
4. Remove from heat and set aside. Flip each tomato half and brush with olive oil garlic mixture and top with grated parmesan cheese.
5. Close griddle and cook for 7-10 minutes more until cheese is melted.
6. Remove tomatoes from the griddle and serve immediately.

NUTRITION: Calories: 130 Fat: 8g Carbs: 9g Protein: 6g

Feta Spinach Turkey Burgers

Preparation Time: 10 minutes

Cooking Time: 10 minutes

Servings: 4

INGREDIENTS:

- 1 lb. Ground turkey
- 1 tbsp. Breadcrumbs
- 1/4 tsp. Crushed red pepper
- 1 tsp. Parsley
- 1 tsp. Oregano
- 1 tsp. Garlic powder
- 1/3 cup. Sun-dried tomatoes
- 1/2 cup, crumbled Feta cheese
- 1/2 cup, chopped Baby spinach
- 1/2 tsp. Pepper
- 1/2 tsp. Sea salt
- Intolerances:
- Egg-Free

DIRECTIONS:

1. Add all ingredients into the mixing bowl and mix until just combined.
2. Make four equal shaped patties from the mixture.
3. Preheat the griddle to high heat.
4. Place patties on a hot griddle and cook for 3-5 minutes on each side or until internal temperature reaches to 165ºF.
5. Serve

NUTRITION: Calories: 215 Fat: 6g Carbs: 9g Protein: 30g

Griddle Potato Skewers

Preparation Time: 15 minutes
Cooking Time: 25 minutes
Servings: 8

INGREDIENTS:

- 2 lbs. quartered Potatoes
- 1 tsp. Garlic powder
- 2 tsps. Crushed dried rosemary
- 4 tbsps. Dry white wine
- 1/2 cup Mayonnaise
- 1/2 cup Water
- Intolerances:
- Gluten-Free
- Egg-Free
- Lactose-Free

DIRECTIONS:

1. Add potatoes and water in a microwave-safe bowl and cook in the microwave for 15 minutes or until potatoes are tender.
2. Drain potatoes well and let them cool. In a large mixing bowl, stir together mayonnaise, garlic powder, rosemary, and wine.
3. Add potatoes and toss to coat. Cover bowl and place in the refrigerator for 1 hour.
4. Preheat the griddle to a high heat and oil grates. Remove potatoes from the marinade and thread onto the skewers.
5. Place potato skewers on a hot griddle, cover, and cook for 6-8 minutes. Turn skewers halfway through.
6. Serve.

NUTRITION: Calories: 135 Fat: 5g Carbs: 20g Protein: 2g

Curried Cauliflower Skewers

Preparation Time: 15 minutes
Cooking Time: 15 minutes
Servings: 6

INGREDIENTS:

- 1 cut into florets large cauliflower head
- 1 cut into wedges onion
- 1 cut into squares yellow bell pepper
- 1 fresh lemon juice
- 1/4 cup olive oil
- 1/2 tsp. garlic powder
- 1/2 tsp. ground ginger
- 3 tsps. curry powder
- 1/2 tsp. salt
- Intolerances:
- Gluten-Free
- Egg-Free
- Lactose-Free

DIRECTIONS:

1. In a large mixing bowl, whisk together oil, lemon juice, garlic, ginger, curry powder, and salt. Add cauliflower florets and toss until well coated.
2. Heat the griddle to medium heat.
3. Thread cauliflower florets, onion, and bell pepper onto the skewers.
4. Place skewers onto the hot griddle and cook for 6-7 minutes on each side.
5. Serve.

NUTRITION: Calories: 100 Fat: 8g Carbs: 6g Protein: 1g

Southwest Chicken Drumsticks

Preparation Time: 10 minutes
Cooking Time: 30 minutes
Servings: 8

INGREDIENTS:

- 2 lbs. Chicken legs
- 2 tbsps. Taco seasoning
- 2 tbsps. Olive oil
- Intolerances:
- Gluten-Free
- Egg-Free
- Lactose-Free

DIRECTIONS:

1. Preheat the griddle to a medium-high heat and oil grates.
2. Brush chicken legs with oil and rub with taco seasoning.
3. Place chicken legs on the hot griddle and cook for 30 minutes.
4. Turn chicken legs after every 10 minutes.
5. Serve.

NUTRITION: Calories: 165 Fat: 12g Carbs: 1g Protein: 10g

Sweet Potato Fries

Preparation Time: 10 minutes
Cooking Time: 12 minutes
Servings: 4

INGREDIENTS:

- 2 lbs. peeled and cut into ½-inch wedges Sweet potatoes
- 2 tbsps. Olive oil
- Pepper and salt to taste
- Intolerances:
- Gluten-Free
- Egg-Free
- Lactose-Free

DIRECTIONS:

1. Preheat the griddle to medium-high heat.
2. Toss sweet potatoes with oil, pepper, and salt.
3. Place sweet potato wedges on a hot griddle and cook over a medium heat for 6 minutes.
4. Flip and cook for 6-8 minutes more.
5. Serve.

NUTRITION: Calories: 230 Fat: 6g Carbs: 40g Protein: 4g

Balsamic Mushroom Skewers

Preparation Time: 10 minutes
Cooking Time: 10 minutes
Servings: 4

INGREDIENTS:

- 2 lbs. sliced ¼-inch thick Mushrooms
- 1/2 tsp. chopped Thyme
- 3 chopped Garlic cloves
- 1 tbsp. Soy sauce
- 2 tbsps. Balsamic vinegar
- Pepper and salt to taste
- Intolerances:
- Gluten-Free
- Egg-Free
- Lactose-Free

DIRECTIONS:

1. Add mushrooms and remaining ingredients into the mixing bowl, cover, and place in the refrigerator for 30 minutes.
2. Thread marinated mushrooms onto the skewers.
3. Heat the griddle to medium-high heat. Place mushroom skewers onto the hot griddle and cook for 2-3 minutes per side.
4. Serve.

NUTRITION: Calories: 60 Fat: 1g Carbs: 8g Protein: 6g

DESSERT AND SNACKS RECIPES

Spicy Sausage & Cheese Balls

Preparation Time: 20 minutes

Cooking Time: 40 minutes

Servings: 4

INGREDIENTS:

- 1lb Hot Breakfast Sausage
- 2 cups Bisquick Baking Mix
- 8 ounces Cream Cheese
- 8 ounces Extra Sharp Cheddar Cheese
- 1/4 cup Fresno Peppers
- 1 tablespoon Dried Parsley
- 1 teaspoon Killer Hogs AP Rub
- 1/2 teaspoon Onion Powder

DIRECTIONS:

1. Get ready griddle or flame broil for roundabout cooking at 400-degree F.
2. Blend Sausage, Baking Mix, destroyed cheddar, cream cheddar, and remaining fixings in a huge bowl until all-around fused.
3. Utilize a little scoop to parcel blend into chomp to estimate balls and roll tenderly fit as a fiddle.
4. Spot wiener and cheddar balls on a cast-iron container and cook for 15mins.
5. Present with your most loved plunging sauces.

NUTRITION: Calories: 95 Carbs: 4g Fat: 7g Protein: 5g

White Chocolate Bread Pudding

Preparation Time: 20 minutes

Cooking Time: 1hr 15 minutes

Servings: 12

INGREDIENTS:

- 1 loaf French bread
- 4 cups Heavy Cream
- 3 Large Eggs
- 2 cups White Sugar
- 1 package White Chocolate morsels
- ¼ cup Melted Butter
- 2 teaspoons Vanilla
- 1 teaspoon Ground Nutmeg
- 1 teaspoon Salt
- Bourbon White Chocolate Sauce
- 1 package White Chocolate morsels
- 1 cup Heavy Cream
- 2 tablespoons Melted Butter
- 2 tablespoons Bourbon
- ½ teaspoon Salt

DIRECTIONS:

1. Preheat the griddle at 350-degree F.

2. Tear French bread into little portions and spot in a massive bowl. Pour four cups of Heavy Cream over Bread and douse for 30mins.

3. Join eggs, sugar, softened spread, and vanilla in a medium to estimate bowl. Include a package of white chocolate pieces and a delicate blend. Season with Nutmeg and Salt.

4. Pour egg combo over the splashed French bread and blend to sign up for.

5. Pour the combination right into a properly to buttered nine X 13 to inchmeal dish and spot it at the griddle.

6. Cook for 60Secs or until bread pudding has set and the top is darker.

7. For the sauce: Melt margarine in a saucepot over medium warm temperature. Add whiskey and hold on cooking for three to 4mins until liquor vanished and margarine begins to darkish-colored.

8. Include vast cream and heat till a mild stew. Take from the warmth and consist of white chocolate pieces a bit at a time continuously blending until the complete percent has softened. Season with a hint of salt and serve over bread pudding.

NUTRITION: Calories: 372 Carbs: 31g Fat: 25g Protein: 5g

Cheesy Jalapeño Griddle Dip

Preparation Time: 10 minutes
Cooking Time: 15 minutes
Servings: 8

INGREDIENTS:

- 8 ounces cream cheese
- 16 ounces shredded cheese
- 1/3 cup mayonnaise
- 4 ounces diced green chilies
- 3 fresh jalapeños
- 2 teaspoons Killer Hogs AP Rub
- 2 teaspoons Mexican Style Seasoning
- For the topping:
- ¼ cup Mexican Blend Shredded Cheese
- Sliced jalapeños
- Mexican Style Seasoning
- 3 tablespoons Killer Hogs AP Rub
- 2 tablespoons Chili Powder
- 2 tablespoons Paprika
- 2 teaspoons Cumin
- ½ teaspoon Granulated Onion
- ¼ teaspoon Cayenne Pepper
- ¼ teaspoon Chipotle Chili Pepper ground
- ¼ teaspoon Oregano

DIRECTIONS:

1. Preheat griddle or flame broil for roundabout cooking at 350 degree
2. Join fixings in a big bowl and spot in a cast to press griddle
3. Top with Mexican Blend destroyed cheddar and cuts of jalapeno's
4. Spot iron griddle on flame broil mesh and cook until cheddar hot and bubbly and the top has seared
5. Marginally about 25mins.
6. Serve warm with enormous corn chips (scoops), tortilla chips, or your preferred vegetables for plunging.

NUTRITION: Calories: 150 Carbs: 22g Fat: 6g Protein: 3g

Cajun Turkey Club

Preparation Time: 5 Minutes
Cooking Time: 10 Minutes
Servings: 3

INGREDIENTS:

- 1 3lbs Turkey Breast
- 1 stick Butter (melted)
- 8 ounces Chicken Broth
- 1 tablespoon Killer Hogs Hot Sauce
- 1/4 cup Malcolm's King Craw Seasoning
- 8 Pieces to Thick Sliced Bacon
- 1 cup Brown Sugar
- 1 head Green Leaf Lettuce
- 1 Tomato (sliced)
- 6 slices Toasted Bread

- ½ cup Cajun Mayo
- 1 cup Mayo
- 1 tablespoon Dijon Mustard
- 1 tablespoon Killer Hogs Sweet Fire Pickles (chopped)
- 1 tablespoon Horseradish
- ½ teaspoon Malcolm's King Craw Seasoning
- 1 teaspoon Killer Hogs Hot Sauce
- Pinch of Salt & Black Pepper to taste

DIRECTIONS:

1. Preheat the griddle 325-degree F

2. Join dissolved margarine, chicken stock, hot sauce, and 1 tbsp of Cajun Seasoning in a blending bowl. Infuse the blend into the turkey bosom scattering the infusion destinations for even inclusion.

3. Shower the outside of the turkey bosom with a Vegetable cooking splash and season with Malcolm's King Craw Seasoning.

4. Spot the turkey bosom on the griddle and cook until the inside temperature arrives at 165 degree. Utilize a moment read thermometer to screen temp during the cooking procedure.

5. Consolidate darker sugar and 1 teaspoon of King Craw in a little bowl. Spread the bacon with the sugar blend and spot on a cooling rack.

6. Cook the bacon for 12 to 15mins or until darker. Make certain to turn the bacon part of the way through for cooking.

7. Toast the bread, cut the tomatoes dainty, and wash/dry the lettuce leaves.

8. At the point when the turkey bosom arrives at 165 take it from the flame broil and rest for 15mins. Take the netting out from around the bosom and cut into slender cuts.

9. To cause the sandwich: To slather Cajun Mayo* on the toast, stack on a few cuts of turkey bosom, lettuce, tomato, and bacon. Include another bit of toast and rehash a similar procedure. Include the top bit of toast slathered with more Cajun mayo, cut the sandwich into equal parts and appreciate.

NUTRITION: Calories: 130 Carbs: 1g Fat: 4g Protein: 21g

Juicy Loosey Cheeseburger

Preparation Time: 10 minutes
Cooking Time: 10 minutes
Servings: 6

INGREDIENTS:

- 2 lbs. ground beef
- 1 egg beaten
- 1 Cup dry bread crumbs
- 3 tablespoons evaporated milk
- 2 tablespoons Worcestershire sauce
- 1 tablespoon Griddle Griddles All Purpose Rub
- 4 slices of cheddar cheese
- 4 buns

DIRECTIONS:

1. Start by consolidating the hamburger, egg, dissipated milk, Worcestershire and focus on a bowl. Utilize your hands to blend well. Partition this blend into 4 equivalent parts. At that point take every one of the 4 sections and partition them into equal parts. Take every one of these little parts and smooth them. The objective is to have 8 equivalent level patties that you will at that point join into 4 burgers.

2. When you have your patties smoothed, place your cheddar in the center and afterward place the other patty over this and firmly squeeze the sides to seal. You may even need to push the meat back towards the inside a piece to shape a marginally thicker patty. The patties ought to be marginally bigger than a standard burger bun as they will recoil a bit of during cooking.

3. Preheat your Kong to 300 degree.

4. Keep in mind during flame broiling that you fundamentally have two meager patties, one on each side, so the cooking time ought not to have a place. You will cook these for 5 to 8mins per side—closer to 5mins on the off chance that you favor an uncommon burger or more towards 8mins in the event that you like a well to done burger.

5. At the point when you flip the burgers, take a toothpick and penetrate the focal point of the burger to permit steam to getaway. This will shield you from having a hit to out or having a visitor who gets a jaw consume from liquid cheddar as they take their first nibble.

6. Toss these on a pleasant roll and top with fixings that supplement whatever your burgers are loaded down with.

NUTRITION: Calories: 300 Carbs: 33g Fat: 12g Protein: 15g

No Flip Burgers

Preparation Time: 30 minutes
Cooking Time: 30 minutes
Servings: 2

INGREDIENTS:

- Ground Beef Patties
- Griddle Griddles Beef Rub
- Choice of Cheese
- Choice of Toppings
- Pretzel Buns

DIRECTIONS:

1. To start, you'll need to begin with freezing yet not solidified meat patties. This will help guarantee that you don't overcook your burgers. Liberally sprinkle on our Beef Rub or All to Purpose Rub and delicately knead into the two sides of the patty. As another option, you can likewise season with salt and pepper and some garlic salt.
2. Preheat your Silverbac to 250-degree Fahrenheit and cook for about 45mins. Contingent upon the thickness of your burgers you will need to keep an eye on them after around 30 to 45mins, yet there's no compelling reason to flip. For a medium to uncommon burger, we recommend cooking to about 155 degree.
3. After the initial 30 to 40mins, in the event that you like liquefied cheddar on your burger feel free to mix it up. Close your barbecue back up and let them wrap up for another 10mins before evacuating. For an additional punch of flavor, finish your burger off with a sprinkle of Griddle Griddle's Gold 'N Bold sauce. Appreciate.

NUTRITION: Calories: 190 Carbs: 17g Fat: 9g Protein: 13g

Juicy Loosey Smokey Burger

Preparation Time: 30 minutes
Cooking Time: 30 minutes
Servings: 2

INGREDIENTS:

- 1-pound Beef
- 1/3 pound per burger
- Cheddar cheese
- Griddle AP Rub
- Salt
- Freshly Ground Black Pepper
- Hamburger Bun
- BBQ Sauce

DIRECTIONS:

1. Split every 1/3 pound of meat, which is 2.66 ounces per half.
2. Level out one half to roughly six inches plate. Put wrecked of American cheddar, leaving 1/2 inch clear.
3. Put another portion of the meat on top, and seal edges. Rehash for all burgers.
4. Sprinkle with Griddle AP rub, salt, and pepper flame broil seasonings.
5. Smoke at 250 for 50mins. No compelling reason to turn.
6. Apply Smokey Dokey BBQ sauce, ideally a mustard-based sauce like Griddle Gold and Bold, or Sticky Fingers Carolina Classic. Cook for an extra 10 minutes, or to favored doneness.

NUTRITION: Calories: 264 Carbs: 57g Fat: 2g Protein: 4g

Bread Pudding

Preparation Time: 15 minutes
Cooking Time: 45 minutes
Servings: 4

INGREDIENTS:

- 8 stale donuts
- 3 eggs
- 1 cup milk
- 1 cup heavy cream
- ½ cup brown sugar
- 1 teaspoon vanilla
- 1 pinch salt
- Blueberry Compote
- 1-pint blueberries
- 2/3 cup granulated sugar
- ¼ cup water
- 1 lemon
- Oat Topping
- 1 cup quick oats
- ½ cup brown sugar
- 1 teaspoon flour
- 2 to 3 tablespoons room temperature butter

DIRECTIONS:

1.   Warmth your Griddle to 350 degree.

2.   Cut your doughnuts into 6 pieces for every doughnut and put it in a safe spot. Blend your eggs, milk, cream, darker sugar, vanilla, and salt in a bowl until it's everything fused. Spot your doughnuts in a lubed 9 by 13 containers at that point pour your custard blend over the doughnuts. Press down on the doughnuts to guarantee they get covered well and absorb the juices.

3.   In another bowl, consolidate your oats, dark colored sugar, flour and gradually join the spread with your hand until the blend begins to cluster up like sand. When that is **Prepared**, sprinkle it over the highest point of the bread pudding and toss it on the barbecue around 40 to 45mins until it gets decent and brilliant dark-colored.

4.   While the bread pudding is **Prepared**, place your blueberries into a griddle over medium-high warmth and begin to cook them down so the juices begin to stream. When that occurs, include your sugar and water and blend well. Diminish the warmth to drug low and let it cool down until it begins to thicken up. Right when the blend begins to thicken, pizzazz your lemon and add the get-up-and-go to the blueberry compote and afterward cut your lemon down the middle and squeeze it into the blend. What you're left with is a tasty, splendid compote that is ideal for the sweetness of the bread pudding.

5.   Watch out for your bread pudding around the 40 to 50mins mark. The blend will, in any case, shake a piece in the middle however will solidify as it stands once you pull it off. You can pull it early on the off chance that you like your bread pudding more sodden however to me, the ideal bread pudding will be dimmer with some caramelization yet will at present have dampness too!

6.   Presently this is the point at which I'd snatch an attractive bowl, toss a pleasant aiding of bread pudding in there then top it off with the compote and a stacking scoop of vanilla bean frozen yogurt at that point watch faces light up. In addition to the fact that this is an amazingly beautiful dish, the flavor will take you out. Destined to be an enormous hit in your family unit. Give it a shot and express gratitude toward me.

7.   What's more, as usual, ensure you snap a photo of your manifestations and label us in your dishes! We'd love to include your work.

NUTRITION: Calories: 290 Carbs: 62g Fat: 4g Protein: 5g

Smoked Chocolate Bacon Pecan Pie

Preparation Time: 1hr 45 minutes

Cooking Time: 45 minutes

Servings: 8

INGREDIENTS:

- 4 eggs
- 1 cup chopped pecans
- 1 tablespoon of vanilla
- ½ cup semi to sweet chocolate chips
- ½ cup dark corn syrup
- ½ cup light corn syrup
- ¾ cup bacon (crumbled)
- ¼ cup bourbon
- 4 tablespoons or ¼ cup of butter
- ½ cup brown sugar
- ½ cup white sugar
- 1 tablespoon cornstarch
- 1 package refrigerated pie dough
- 16 ounces heavy cream
- ¾ cup white sugar
- ¼ cup bacon
- 1 tablespoon vanilla

DIRECTIONS:

1. Pie:
2. Carry Griddle to 350 degree.
3. Blend 4 tablespoons spread, ½ cup darker sugar, and ½ cup white sugar in blending bowl.
4. In a different bowl, blend 4 eggs and 1 tablespoon cornstarch together and add to blender.
5. Include ½ cup dull corn syrup, ½ cup light corn syrup, ¼ cup whiskey, 1 cup slashed walnuts, 1 cup bacon, and 1 tablespoon vanilla to blend.
6. Spot pie batter in 9-inch pie griddle.
7. Daintily flour mixture.
8. Uniformly place ½ cup chocolate contributes pie dish.
9. Take blend into the pie dish.
10. Smoke at 350 degree for 40mins or until the focus is firm.
11. Cool and top with bacon whipped cream.
12. Bacon whipped Cream:
13. Consolidate fixings (16 ounces substantial cream, ¾ cup white sugar, ¼ cup bacon to finely cleaved, and 1 tablespoon vanilla) and mix at rapid until blend thickens. This formula can be separated into 6mins pie container or custard dishes or filled in as one entire pie.

NUTRITION: Calories: 200 Carbs: 18g Fat: 0g Protein: 3g

Bacon Sweet Potato Pie

Preparation Time: 15 minutes
Cooking Time: 50 minutes
Servings: 8

INGREDIENTS:

- 1 pound 3 ounces sweet potatoes
- 1 ¼ cups plain yogurt
- ¾ cup packed, dark brown sugar
- ½ teaspoon of cinnamon
- ¼ teaspoon of nutmeg
- 5 egg yolks
- ¼ teaspoon of salt
- 1 (up to 9 inch) deep dish, frozen pie shell
- 1 cup chopped pecans, toasted
- 4 strips of bacon, cooked and diced
- 1 tablespoon maple syrup
- Optional: Whipped topping

DIRECTIONS:

1. In the first region, 3D shapes the potatoes right into a steamer crate and sees into a good-sized pot of stew water. Ensure the water is not any nearer than creeps from the base of the bushel. When steamed for 20mins, pound with a potato masher and installed a safe spot.

2. While your flame broil is preheating, location the sweet potatoes within the bowl of a stand blender and beat with the oar connection.

3. Include yogurt, dark colored sugar, cinnamon, nutmeg, yolks, and salt, to flavor, and beat until very a whole lot joined. Take this hitter into the pie shell and see onto a sheet dish. Sprinkle walnuts and bacon on pinnacle and bathe with maple syrup.

4. Heat for 45 to 60mins or until the custard arrives at 165 to 180 degree. Take out from fish fry and funky. Keep refrigerated within the wake of cooling.

NUTRITION: Calories: 270 Carbs: 39g Fat: 12g Protein: 4g

Griddle Fruit with Cream

Preparation Time: 15 minutes

Cooking Time: 10 minutes

Servings: 6

INGREDIENTS:

- 2 halved Apricot
- 1 halved Nectarine
- 2 halved peaches
- ¼ cup of Blueberries
- ½ cup of Raspberries
- 2 tablespoons of Honey
- 1 orange, the peel
- 2 cups of Cream
- ½ cup of Balsamic Vinegar

DIRECTIONS:

1. Preheat the griddle to 400F with closed lid.

2. Griddle the peaches, nectarines and apricots for 4 minutes on each side.

3. Place a pan over the stove and turn on medium heat. Add 2 tablespoons of honey, vinegar, and orange peel. Simmer until medium thick.

4. In the meantime, add honey and cream in a bowl. Whip until it reaches a soft form.

5. Place the fruits on a serving plate. Sprinkle with berries. Drizzle with balsamic reduction. Serve with cream and enjoy!

NUTRITION: Calories: 230 Protein: 3g Carbs: 35g Fat: 3g

Apple Pie on the Griddle

Preparation Time: 15 minutes
Cooking Time: 30 minutes
Servings: 6

INGREDIENTS:

- ¼ cup of Sugar
- 4 Apples, sliced
- 1 tablespoon of Cornstarch
- 1 teaspoon Cinnamon, ground
- 1 Pie Crust, refrigerated, soften in according to the directions on the box
- ½ cup of Peach preserves

DIRECTIONS:

1. Preheat the griddle to 375F with closed lid.
2. In a bowl combine the cinnamon, cornstarch, sugar, and apples. Set aside.
3. Place the piecrust in a pie pan. Spread the preserves and then place the apples. Fold the crust slightly.
4. Place a pan on the griddle (upside - down) so that you don't brill/bake the pie directly on the heat.
5. Cook 30 - 40 minutes. Once done, set aside to rest. Serve and enjoy

NUTRITION: Calories: 160 Protein: 0.5g Carbs: 35g Fat: 1g

Griddle Layered Cake

Preparation Time: 10 minutes
Cooking Time: 20 minutes
Servings: 6

INGREDIENTS:

- 2 x pound cake
- 3 cups of whipped cream
- ¼ cup melted butter
- 1 cup of blueberries
- 1 cup of raspberries
- 1 cup sliced strawberries

DIRECTIONS:

1. Preheat the griddle to high with closed lid.
2. Slice the cake loaf (3/4 inch), about 10 per loaf. Brush both sides with butter.
3. Griddle for 7 minutes on each side. Set aside.
4. Once cooled completely start layering your cake. Place cake, berries then cream.
5. Sprinkle with berries and serve.

NUTRITION: Calories: 160 Protein: 2.3g Carbs: 22g Fat: 6g

Coconut Chocolate Simple Brownies

Preparation Time: 15 minutes
Cooking Time: 25 minutes
Servings: 6

INGREDIENTS:

- 4 eggs
- 1 cup Cane Sugar
- ¾ cup of Coconut oil
- 4 ounces chocolate, chopped
- ½ teaspoon of Sea salt
- ¼ cup cocoa powder, unsweetened
- ½ cup flour
- 4 ounces Chocolate chips
- 1 teaspoon of Vanilla

DIRECTIONS:

1. Preheat the griddle to 350F with closed lid.
2. Take a baking pan (9x9), grease it and line a parchment paper.
3. In a bowl combine the salt, cocoa powder and flour. Stir and set aside.
4. In the microwave or double boiler melt the coconut oil and chopped chocolate. Let it cool a bit.
5. Add the vanilla, eggs, and sugar. Whisk to combine.
6. Add into the flour, and add chocolate chips. Pour the mixture into a pan.
7. Place the pan on the grate. Bake for 20 minutes. If you want dryer brownies to bake for 5 - 10 minutes more.
8. Let them cool before cutting.
9. Cut the brownies into squares and serve.

NUTRITION: Calories: 135 Protein: 2g Carbs: 16g Fat: 3g

Seasonal Fruit on the Griddle

Preparation Time: 5 minutes
Cooking Time: 10 minutes
Servings: 4

INGREDIENTS:

- 2 plums, peaches apricots, etc. (choose seasonally)
- 3 tablespoons Sugar, turbinate
- ¼ cup of Honey
- Gelato, as desired

DIRECTIONS:

1. Preheat the griddle to 450F with closed lid.
2. Slice each fruit in halves and remove pits. Brush with honey. Sprinkle with some sugar.
3. Griddle on the grate until you see that there are griddle marks. Set aside.
4. Serve each with a scoop of gelato. Enjoy.

NUTRITION: Calories: 120 Protein: 1g Carbs: 15g Fat: 3g

Bacon Chocolate Chip Cookies

Preparation Time: 30 minutes
Cooking Time: 30 minutes
Servings: 6

INGREDIENTS:

- 8 slices cooked and crumbled bacon
- 2 ½ teaspoon apple cider vinegar
- 1 teaspoon vanilla
- 2 cup semisweet chocolate chips
- 2 room temp eggs
- 1 ½ teaspoon baking soda
- 1 cup granulated sugar
- ½ teaspoon salt
- 2 ¾ cup all-purpose flour
- 1 cup light brown sugar
- 1 ½ stick softened butter

DIRECTIONS:

1. Mix salt, baking soda and flour.
2. Cream the sugar and the butter together. Lower the speed. Add in the eggs, vinegar, and vanilla.
3. Put it on low fire, slowly add in the flour mixture, bacon pieces, and chocolate chips.
4. Preheat your griddle, with your lid closed, until it reaches 375.
5. Put a parchment paper on a baking sheet you are using and drop a teaspoonful of cookie batter on the baking sheet. Let them cook on the griddle, covered, for approximately 12 minutes or until they are browned.

NUTRITION: Calories: 167 Carbs: 21g Fat: 9g Protein: 2g

Chocolate Chip Cookies

Preparation Time: 30 minutes
Cooking Time: 30 minutes
Servings: 8

INGREDIENTS:

- 1 ½ cup chopped walnuts
- 1 teaspoon vanilla
- 2 cup chocolate chips
- 1 teaspoon baking soda
- 2 ½ cup plain flour
- ½ teaspoon salt
- 1 ½ stick softened butter
- 2 eggs
- 1 cup brown sugar
- ½ cup sugar

DIRECTIONS:

1. Preheat your griddle, with your lid closed, until it reaches 350.
2. Mix the baking soda, salt, and flour.
3. Cream the brown sugar, sugar, and butter. Mix in the vanilla and eggs until it comes together.
4. Slowly add in the flour while continuing to beat. Once all flour has been incorporated, add in the chocolate chips and walnuts. Using a spoon, fold into batter.
5. Place an aluminum foil onto griddle. In an aluminum foil, drop spoonful of dough and bake for 17 minutes.

NUTRITION: Calories: 150 Carbs: 18g Fat: 5g Protein: 10g

Apple Cobbler

Preparation Time: 30 minutes
Cooking Time: 1 hour 50 minutes
Servings: 8

INGREDIENTS:

- 8 Granny Smith apples
- 1 cup sugar
- 1 stick melted butter
- 1 teaspoon cinnamon
- Pinch salt
- ½ cup brown sugar
- 2 eggs
- 2 teaspoons baking powder
- 2 cup plain flour
- 1 ½ cup sugar

DIRECTIONS:

1. Peel and quarter apples, place into a bowl. Add in the cinnamon and one c. sugar. Stir well to coat and let it set for one hour.
2. Preheat your griddle, with your lid closed, until it reaches 350.
3. In a large bowl add the salt, baking powder, eggs, brown sugar, sugar, and flour. Mix until it forms crumbles.
4. Place apples into rack Add the crumble mixture on top and drizzle with melted butter.
5. Place on the griddle and cook for 50 minutes.

NUTRITION: Calories: 152 Carbs: 26g Fat: 5g Protein: 1g

Caramel Bananas

Preparation Time: 15 minutes.

Cooking Time: 15 minutes.

Servings: 4

INGREDIENTS:

- 1/3 cup chopped pecans
- ½ cup sweetened condensed milk
- 4 slightly green bananas
- ½ cup brown sugar
- 2 tablespoons corn syrup
- ½ cup butter

DIRECTIONS:

1. Preheat your griddle, with the lid closed, until it reaches 350.

2. Place the milk, corn syrup, butter, and brown sugar into a heavy saucepan and bring to boil. For five minutes simmer the mixture in low heat. Stir frequently.

3. Place the bananas with their peels on, on the griddle and let them griddle for five minutes. Flip and cook for five minutes more. Peels will be dark and might split.

4. Place on serving platter. Cut the ends off the bananas and split peel down the middle. Take the peel off the bananas and spoon caramel on top. Sprinkle with pecans.

NUTRITION: Calories: 152 Carbs: 36g Fat: 1g Protein: 1g

Cinnamon Sugar Pumpkin Seeds

Preparation Time: 15 minutes

Cooking Time: 30 minutes

Servings: 8

INGREDIENTS:

- 2 tablespoons sugar
- Seeds from a pumpkin
- 1 teaspoon cinnamon
- 2 tablespoons melted butter

DIRECTIONS:

1. Preheat your griddle, with your lid closed, until it reaches 350.

2. Clean the seeds and toss them in the melted butter. Add them to the sugar and cinnamon. Spread them out on a baking sheet, place on the griddle, and smoke for 25 minutes. Serve.

NUTRITION: Calories: 127 Protein: 5g Carbs: 15g Fat: 21g

Blackberry Pie

Preparation Time: 15 minutes

Cooking Time: 40 minutes

Servings: 8

INGREDIENTS:

- Butter, for greasing
- ½ cup all-purpose flour
- ½ cup milk
- 2 pints blackberries
- 2 cup sugar, divided
- 1 box refrigerated piecrusts
- 1 stick melted butter
- 1 stick of butter
- Vanilla ice cream

DIRECTIONS:

1. Preheat your griddle, with your lid closed, until it reaches 375.
2. Butter a cast iron griddle.
3. Unroll a piecrust and lay it in the bottom and up the sides of the griddle. Use a fork to poke holes in the crust.
4. Lay the griddle on the griddle and smoke for five mins, or until the crust is browned. Set off the griddle.
5. Mix together 1 ½ c. of sugar, the flour, and the melted butter together. Add in the blackberries and toss everything together.
6. The berry mixture should be added to the griddle. The milk should be added on the top afterward. Sprinkle on half of the diced butter.
7. Unroll the second pie crust and lay it over the griddle. You can also slice it into strips and weave it on top to make it look like a lattice. Place the rest of the diced butter over the top. Sprinkle the rest of the sugar over the crust and place it griddle back on the griddle.
8. Lower the lid and smoke for 15 to 20 minutes or until it is browned and bubbly. You may want to cover with some foil to keep it from burning during the last few minutes of cooking. Serve the hot pie with some vanilla ice cream.

NUTRITION: Calories: 393 Protein 4.25g Carbs: 53.67g Fat: 18.75g

S'mores Dip

Preparation Time: 10 minutes
Cooking Time: 25 minutes
Servings: 8

INGREDIENTS:

- 12 ounces semisweet chocolate chips
- ¼ cup milk
- 2 tablespoons melted salted butter
- 16 ounces marshmallows
- Apple wedges
- Graham crackers

DIRECTIONS:

1. Preheat your griddle, with your lid closed, until it reaches 450.
2. Put a cast iron griddle on your griddle and add in the milk and melted butter. Stir together for a minute.
3. Once it has heated up, top with the chocolate chips, making sure it makes a single layer. Place the marshmallows on top, standing them on their end and covering the chocolate.
4. Cover, and let it smoke for five to seven minutes. The marshmallows should be toasted lightly.
5. Take the griddle off the heat and serve with apple wedges and graham crackers.

NUTRITION: Calories: 216.7 Protein 2.7g Carbs: 41g Fat: 4.7g

Ice Cream Bread

Preparation Time: 10 minutes
Cooking Time: 1 hour
Servings: 6

INGREDIENTS:

- 1 ½ quart full-fat butter pecan ice cream, softened
- 1 teaspoon salt
- 2 cups semisweet chocolate chips
- 1 cup sugar
- 1 stick melted butter
- Butter, for greasing
- 4 cups self-rising flour

DIRECTIONS:

1. Preheat your griddle, with your lid closed, until it reaches 350.
2. Mix together the salt, sugar, flour, and ice cream with an electric mixer set to medium for two minutes.
3. As the mixer is still running, add in the chocolate chips, beating until everything is blended.
4. Spray a Bundt pan or tube pan with cooking spray. If you choose to use a pan that is solid, the center will take too long to cook. That's why a tube or Bundt pan works best.
5. Add the batter to your **Prepared** pan.
6. Set the cake on the griddle, cover, and smoke for 50 minutes to an hour. A toothpick should come out clean.
7. Take the pan off of the griddle. For 10 minutes cool the bread. Remove carefully the bread from the pan and then drizzle it with some melted butter.

NUTRITION: Calories: 148.7 Protein: 3.5g Carbs: 27g Fat: 3g

30 DAY MEAL PLAN

DAY	BREAKFAST	MAINS	DESSERTS AND SNACKS
1	Almond Pancakes	Pork Tenderloin Sandwiches	Spicy Sausage & Cheese Balls
2	French Toast Sticks	Herb-Crusted Mediterranean Pork Tenderloin	White Chocolate Bread Pudding
3	Simple Cheese Sandwich	Paprika Dijon Pork Tenderloin	Cheesy Jalapeño Griddle Dip
4	Cauliflower Fritters	Moroccan Spiced Pork Tenderloin with Creamy Harissa Sauce	Cajun Turkey Club
5	Easy Banana Pancakes	Sticky-Sweet Pork Shoulder	Juicy Loosey Cheeseburger
6	Cauliflower Hash Browns	Griddle Pork Chops with Herb Apple Compote	No Flip Burgers
7	Tomato Scrambled Egg	Yucatan-Style Griddle Pork	Juicy Loosey Smokey Burger
8	Caprese Omelet	Glazed Country Ribs	Bread Pudding
9	Pumpkin Pancake	Pineapple Bacon Pork Chops	Smoked Chocolate Bacon Pecan Pie
10	Easy Cheese Omelet	Habanero-Marinated Pork Chops	Bacon Sweet Potato Pie
11	Spinach Pancakes	Garlic Soy Pork Chops	Griddle Fruit with Cream
12	Spicy Egg Scrambled	Honey Soy Pork Chops	Apple Pie on the Griddle
13	Chocolate Pancake	Cuban Pork Chops	Griddle Layered Cake
14	Broccoli Omelet	Spicy Cajun Pork Chops	Coconut Chocolate Simple Brownies
15	Healthy Oatmeal Pancake	Classic BBQ Chicken	Seasonal Fruit on the Griddle
16	Tangy Chicken Sandwiches	California Seared Chicken	Bacon Chocolate Chip Cookies
17	Sun-Dried Tomato and Chicken Flatbreads	Sweet Chili Lime Chicken	Chocolate Chip Cookies
18	Turkey Pesto Panini	Seared Spicy Citrus Chicken	Apple Cobbler
19	Classic American Burger	Honey Balsamic Marinated Chicken	Caramel Bananas
20	Layered Beef & Corn Burger	Salsa Verde Marinated Chicken	Cinnamon Sugar Pumpkin Seeds

21	Pork Tenderloin Sandwiches	Hasselback Stuffed Chicken	Blackberry Pie
22	Cheesy Ham and Pineapple Sandwich	Creole Chicken Stuffed With Cheese & Peppers	S'mores Dip
23	Croque Madame	Root Beer Can Chicken	Ice Cream Bread
24	Salmon Burgers	Chipotle Adobe Chicken	Spicy Sausage & Cheese Balls
25	Ultimate Griddle Cheese	Chicken Tacos With Avocado Crema	White Chocolate Bread Pudding
26	Garlic Parmesan Griddle Cheese Sandwiches	Sizzling Chicken Fajitas	Cheesy Jalapeño Griddle Dip
27	Griddle Pizza Cheese	Hawaiian Chicken Skewers	Cajun Turkey Club
28	Mini Portobello Burgers	Fiery Italian Chicken Skewers	Juicy Loosey Cheeseburger
29	Veggie Pesto Flatbread	Chicken Thighs With Ginger-Sesame Glaze	No Flip Burgers
30	Griddle Vegetable Pizza	Honey Sriracha Griddle Chicken Thighs	Juicy Loosey Smokey Burger